The Greener Homes Price Guide

Organising and budgeting for energy
efficiency and reducing your carbon footprint

 BCIS is the building cost information service of RICS

The Greener Homes Price Guide

©RICS

ISBN 978 1 904829 67 6

BCIS
12 Great George Street
Parliament Square
London SW1P 3AD
www.bcis.co.uk

BCIS is a trading name of RICS

Printed by Print Direction Ltd, Llanmaes, Wales. www.printdirection.co.uk

Contents

Part One

Part Two

Part Three

Part Four

Glossary

Index

PART ONE

1.1 INTRODUCTION

Your Money and a Greener Home: Does it Work for You?

When making changes to your home there are three issues to consider, other than whether you can afford it:

- Will it reduce my carbon footprint?
- Is it economical, i.e. do the energy savingS repay the initial outlay in a reasonable number of years?
- Will it be disruptive and require other, ancillary, building works?

All the works described in this book will reduce your carbon footprint.

- There are works that are economical and cause little disruption, e.g. changing light fittings.
- There are some that are economical in themselves but are disruptive and are likely to require ancillary works.
- There are those that are marginal in economic terms and cause little disruption.
- There are those that are marginal in economic terms but are disruptive and are likely require ancillary works.
- There are those that are not economical and cause little disruption.
- There are those that are not economical and are disruptive, and are likely to require ancillary works.

Items that are disruptive may become more economically viable if you are carrying out a major intervention in your house for other reasons. So, if you are replacing your roof or boarding your loft, the cost of installing roof insulation as part of this process will be significantly reduced if done at the same time.

There are some works, such as insulation to solid walls, that are only likely to be viable when a house or part of it, is being completely refurbished.

Introducing Realism

What BCIS have sought to do in this publication is to introduce something that has been in scant supply - realism.

We won't tell you that you are going to save lots of money if that really isn't true because that way tarnishes the whole concept of greening your home and undermines the serious effort of addressing carbon emissions.

There are lots of things to test and evaluate and evaluating the impact of the technologies on overall carbon emissions is difficult, but broadly:

Are the changes proposed economically viable?

- There are those things that will save you money.
- There are those things that may save you money.
- There are those things that won't save you money.

There are tried and tested sums to work out the economic viability, based on what interest rate you can get by investing money, that will indicate what payback periods are sensible to invest in.

Will the Changes Reduce Your Carbon Emissions or Carbon Footprint?
- There are those things that have a beneficial impact on carbon emissions.
- There are those where the impact is marginal.
- There are those things that initially might look 'green' but aren't really because they will break and have to be replaced. Anything with moving parts will break and if you don't take into account maintenance, service and replacement, it's arguable whether they are green at all. Many other providers of payback periods have simply not taken into account maintenance, which is a pretty fundamental omission. If the thing is going to break then it's unlikely to have a good payback period or to reduce your carbon footprint.

So you need to decide what your reason for making the change is.

If your reason is to save money then our investigation suggests you should be considering the following areas; laying new or increasing the insulation in the loft, installing double glazing, cavity wall insulation to external walls and fitting thermostatic valves to radiators.

If your reason is to 'save the planet' then you still need to know what the 'cost to you is'. The things that have the most impact on the carbon position are replacing coiled fired or older gas boilers and installing solar and photovoltaic panels, but the economics may not work for you.

Remember 'Some Times Are Better Than Others to be Thinking Green'
What can you do whilst you are doing something else? If you are replacing your boiler, it may well be worth spending a bit more on a boiler that is more efficient?

If you are retiling your loft then insulating it at the same time is the cost of the insulation and a couple of hour's work, but doing it at another time will be a day's work.

If you are going to gut your house then you can include all of the 'green measures' but it will reduce your internal floor area and you need to think carefully about the things that you place on the outside (microgeneration – windturbine/solar).

How Does This Book Help?
This guide will help you if you want to:
- Improve the energy efficiency within your home by saving on wastage.
- Install new equipment to reduce running costs.

There are lots of books available telling you what to do to improve your property, to make it more environmentally friendly, but what they don't usually tell you is what it will really cost. This guide does.

The guide:
- Gives you the cost information that will enable you to budget for improving the energy efficiency of your home and reducing the carbon footprint.

- Walks you through how to obtain builders or specialist contractors to actually do the work.
- Provides an indication of savings in running costs.
- Provides an idea of payback periods.
- Enables you to assess your carbon footprint.

BCIS Star Rating

A star rating system has been included against the priced items in Part 3.

An indication of the value of the work has been rated in four parts as follows:

Box £ – Cost of work as shown in Part 3.
Box P – Payback period (Recovery of cost time).
Box E – Energy savings (carbon dioxide emissions saving).
Box D – Disruptive costs to households whilst work is being carried out.

It is worth noting here that that the energy saving also gives an indication of the carbon dioxide emissions saving. The UK Government publishes conversion factors to determine the carbon dioxide emissions caused by the use of energy. This is, of necessity, an approximation since the actual carbon dioxide emission saving is inherently much more difficult to calculate since it is dependent on such factors as the source of energy used to make materials, where the materials have been transported from, and so on.

The final box gives the overall rating for the item, five stars being the best value for the initial investment and the least disruptive.

The star rating has been assessed on a scale of one to five stars, one star being the dearest, most disruptive, least energy saving and longest time to payback, and five stars being the cheapest, least disruptive, most energy saving, shortest time to payback the initial outlay.

The key for the BCIS Star Rating system is given below and is also reproduced in Part Three itself complete with fuller definitions.

BCIS Star Rating

£ = Cost
More than £10000
£5001 to£ 10000
£1001 to £5000
£501 to £1000
£1 to £500

P = Payback period (recovery of cost time)
More than 100 years
51 years to 100 years
26 to 50 years
11 to 25 years
Up to 10 years

E = Energy saving per year
Up to £25 p.a
£26 to £50 p.a
£51 to £75 p.a.
£76 to £100 p.a.
More than £100 p.a.

D = Disruption
Major disruption to whole house
Major disruption to rooms or part of house
Minor disruption to room/part of house
Little disruption, minor moving and making good
No disruption

Overall = Overall BCIS rating
Poor
Medium
Good
Very Good
Excellent

A Note of Caution for the Uninitiated
If you've watched any of the TV programmes relating to energy savings in homes, you'll know that it is very important to get your budget right before starting any construction project.

Some of the TV programmes only talk about the costs of materials. If you were to run some of these projects yourself, you would need to budget the cost of all those workmen, 'the labour' and what it would cost you to get advice from the 'TV experts'.

This guide gives you advice on:
- The types of work you may need to undertake when upgrading the insulation in a property, together with approximate costs.
- An idea of the cost of improving energy efficiency.
- Guide costs for additions or

improvements to fuel source, such as using gas central heating systems, wind turbines, photovoltaic panels and solar panels.

- Costs for a range of new items to reduce carbon emissions such as wind turbines, photovoltaic panels, solar panels and heat recovery ventilation.
- The possible savings made after the works are completed, together with the payback periods.

There is also guidance on:

- Selecting contractors.
- How to carry out the work.
- Deciding payment - what to pay, to whom and when.
- Changing your mind - what to do if you want to ask for something different to be carried out - variations and extras.

There are common pitfalls in all these areas and this guide will help keep you out of trouble.

You may be able to get grants from your local authority for renovation work. This guide explains the eligibility, the limits and how to apply them. It is worth a look, but the reality is that unless you are on a low income, you are unlikely to be eligible.

Layout of the Guide

The guide is in four parts.

Part One

- Introduction
- Layout of the guide
- How to use the guide
- Cost information.
- How to employ a contractor
- Planning, and building legislation and regulations, to consider before undertaking the work, particularly with regard to works of alteration and new works.
- Party walls, building materials
- Grants and Value Added Tax

Part Two
This part of the guide contains textual information on products available to improve a dwelling.
- Passive Improvements:
  - Insulation
  - Windows
  - Doors
  - Other Works – conservatories and sun lounges, porches, rooflights.

- Replacement of Existing
  - Heating – boilers, radiators
  - Plumbing and Services – hot water pipes and cylinders, cold water pipes and tanks
  - Electrical – lighting, appliances
  - Smart metering
  - Heat pumps
  - Heat recovery ventilation.

- Active Improvements
  - Heating – solar panels, heat pumps
  - Power – photovoltaic panels, wind turbines
  - Combined Heating and Power – photovoltaic and solar roof tiles, microchip combined heat and power
  - Ventilation, Heat Recovery and Comfort Cooling
  - Rainwater harvesting and greywater.

Part Three
This part of the guide contains the cost information on items, including initial installation, running costs and payback periods. The BCIS star rating is included against items in this section.

- Costings
- Payback periods
- Energy savings
- Zero carbon rating

Part Four
- Costing assumptions used in the build up of the prices in this guide.
- General building information.
- Useful contacts.

Glossary – The glossary will help you to talk to the builder. The cost information is described in terms that a builder understands. Of course, this means that there will be some items where you may say 'well what on earth is that'. The glossary will help you to get around this problem.

How to Use the Guide
For any building project you should follow some simple steps:
1. Identify the work required.
2. Consult specialists where appropriate.
3. Produce a budget.
4. Consult a contractor(s).
5. Adjust your budget for any additional work identified.
6. Obtain quotes.
7. Agree a payment schedule.
8. Commence work.

Part 1.2 of the guide shows how the information has been presented and suggests how it can be used.

It is important that you read the Introduction in full before trying to use the costs in this guide on a specific project the energy efficiency of your property.

1.2 COST INFORMATION

About the Cost Information

The cost information in Part 3 is presented in three sections:

1. **Passive Improvements**. This covers improving the insulation levels of a property. This includes roof spaces, external walls, windows and doors, ground floor and pipework. In general, items in this section do not include machinery and require little or no maintenance once installed.

2. **Replacement of Existing Equipment**. This covers the replacement of items normally found in houses such as boilers, water heaters, metering equipment and appliances. In general, items in this section include machinery that requires maintenance once installed.

3. **Active Improvements.** This section provides prices for the installation of solar panels, voltaic panels, heat pumps, and wind turbines. This section deals with the use of rainwater to provide irrigation for gardens and for some internal usage. These items involve the installation of new plant and machinery and have maintenance and service life considerations.

What is Included in the Costs?

The costs given in all the tables include for everything necessary to carry out the works. This includes:

- Labour
- Materials
- Contractors' overheads and profit
- Scaffolding and plant required to carry out the work
- Value Added Tax. This is only included where indicated at the start of the costs.

For small items of work, the costs have also included the contractor's call out charge (see Page 14).

House Sizes

Where the cost is for work to a whole house, three examples are given to indicate the range of likely costs:

- **Terraced**. This refers to a two bedroom terraced house of 21m² area on plan (42m² total on two floors).
- **Semi Detached**. This refers to a three bedroom semi detached property of 42m² area on plan (84m² total on two floors).
- **Detached**. This refers to a detached house of 125m² on plan (250m² on two floors).

Elevation drawings of the houses used are presented in Part 4.

Call out Charges

Contractors will often charge for coming to your house. This is referred to as a 'call out charge'. For small items of work, the call out charge may be more than the cost of carrying out the work. Some contractors will include the first half hour of any work in the call out charge; this is particularly common with 'emergency' services such as drain clearing.

Generally, call out charges have been included in items under £250.

BCIS carried out a survey of contractors' call out charges for this book. Call out charges differ between and within, the trades. Call out charges for a general builder ranged from £15 to £80, plumbers £25 to £55, roofers £45 to £350 and electricians £20 to £80. The costs included in the rates given in the guide are:

- General builder, carpenter, plumber, plasterer, glazier, painter   £50
- Roofer   £175
- Electrician   £35

Where more than one item of work is carried out on a single visit, only one call out charge will apply and you should adjust the costs in the guide accordingly. An example of this adjustment is shown on Page 19.

Where a contractor has quoted for work, the call out charge should be included in his quote.

The Cost Tables
Choosing the costs: The tables show costs for items of works. Against each item, costs are given for a range of quantities.

In the example below, costs for insulation to pipework are given for a number of lengths.

Replace missing or damaged insulation

	Length of Pipework (m)			
Costs include VAT at 17.5%	1	2	5	10
	£	£	£	£
Replace insulation to pipework				
Pipework in roof space or cupboards	73	85	110	170
Pipework under floors				
Pipes running in direction of floor boarding	79	98	145	240
Pipes running in opposite direction to floor boarding	120	175	325	550

Using the Costs from the Tables
Adjusting for quantity: The costs given are for a range of quantities, e.g. in the above example, for 1, 2, 5 and 10m runs of pipework. You may need to adjust these for different quantities. This can be done in two ways:

Applying a unit rate. You can calculate a unit rate cost/m in this example and apply it to the required quantity,

> e.g. replacing 13m of insulation to pipework in roof space:
>
> | 10m costs: | £170 |
> | --- | --- |
> | 1m costs: | $\frac{£170}{10} = £17/m$ |
> | **13m costs:** | **£17/m x 13m = £221** |

Note: If you do the same calculation using the cost of 5m, this estimates the cost of replacing 13m of insulation at £286.

Pro-ratering. Alternatively, for some items where the range of costs is large you may wish to pro rata the costs between the quantities,

> e.g. replacing 4m of insulation to pipework in roof space:

2m costs:	£85	
5m costs:	£110	
3 additional m costs:	£110-£85	= £25
1 additional m costs:	$\frac{£25}{3}$	= £8
2 additional m costs:	£8 x 2	= £16
4m costs:	**£85+16**	**= £101**

If the quantity of work is beyond the scope of the quantities given in a table, an estimate can be made, within reason, by extrapolation,

> e.g. replacing 13m of insulation to pipework in roof space:

10m costs:	£170	
5m costs:	£110	
5 additional m costs:	£170-£110	= £60
1 additional m costs:	$\frac{£60}{5}$	= £12
3 additional m costs:	£12 x 3	= £36
13m costs:	**£170+36**	**= £206**

Adjusting for Location
The cost of building work varies around the country.

The costs in this guide represent UK 'national average costs'. They may need to be adjusted for location, and adjustment factors are provided in Section 4.3.

- If the total cost of the project is less than £1,000 then it is probably not worth adjusting for location.
- For projects likely to cost more than £1,000, it would be worth thinking about the affect of location.

Using the Location Factors

The costs from the tables should be multiplied by the factors for the area where the project is located:

For example, costs in Wales are generally lower than the national average. The location factor for Wales is 0.96. Therefore, a project calculated to cost £20,000 from the table, is likely to cost £20,000 x 0.96 if it is located in Wales = £19,200.

Similarly, it is generally more expensive to build in Greater London. The location factor for London is 1.14. Therefore, a project calculated to cost £100,000 from the table, is likely to cost £20,000 x 1.14 if it is located in London = £22,800.

These adjustment factors relate to the cost of doing work and not the specification of the work. So, adjusting the cost of installing windows to London prices allows for the additional cost of fitting windows of a given standard, it does not allow for the difference in specification that might be appropriate in the different locations.

The location factors also allow comparison of costs between regions. If you know the cost of replacing windows in Wales then you can work out what it might cost in London, as follows:

Known cost of our windows in Wales	= £7,070
Location factor for Wales	= 0.96
Location factor for Greater London	= 1.14
Difference in price between Wales and Greater London	$= \dfrac{1.14}{0.96} = 1.19$
Estimated cost of our windows in Greater London	= £7,070 x 1.19 = £8,420

Rounding

The costs in the tables have been rounded to reflect the nature of the guide. Generally, costs have been rounded as follows:

- Less than £100 — rounded up to the nearest £1, e.g. £51.49 has been shown as £52.
- From £100 to £1000 — rounded up to the nearest £5, e.g. £846 has been shown as £850.
- Greater than £1000 — rounded up to the nearest £10, e.g. £1447 has been shown as £1450.

These rounding conventions are not intended to imply a level of predictive accuracy.

Cost Base and Inflation
The costs in the tables are current at 4th quarter 2007. Adjustments for future inflation can be found in Part 4, where forecasts of costs over the next three years are shown.

Costing Assumptions and Procurement Context
Costs in this guide are for completing the work described as an individual job. They include contractors' overheads, scaffolding where applicable, and VAT where appropriate. They exclude any temporary works, contingencies and any fees that may be applicable. Details of these items are described in Part 4.

Building costs are influenced by a range of factors such as:
* Quantity of work
* When work is carried out
* Availability of space to work and store materials
* Provision of water and power
* The need for scaffolding
* Availability of materials and labour

These factors are the context in which you procure the work.

The costs in this guide are based on the assumptions about the procurement context that are given in the Costing Assumptions in Part 4, together with advice on how they influence costs. You should be aware of these assumptions and adjust the costs where actual circumstances differ.

There is no 'right' cost for building work. It is always an agreed price between a willing seller - the contractor, and a willing buyer - you. When there are shortages of labour, prices will rise, when there is a shortage of work they will go down. In recent years, there has been a shortage of labour, an acute shortage in some areas, but the influx of builders from the new EU member states has helped to ease the situation.

The costs in this guide are intended to be reasonable where there is a sufficient supply of labour.

Costing Repairs – Examples
Example A
Property – 3 bedroom semi detached house.
Replace badly fitting front and back doors.

	£
From Part 3.1 - Passive Improvements – External Doors and Frames. Page 82	
Replace timber door and frame with uPVC door and frame Georgian panelled back door	840
Page 82	
Replace timber door and frame with uPVC door and frame Georgian panelled timber effect front door with glazed opening over	1,300
Total cost of works	£ 2,140
	SAY £2,200

Example B
Property – 4 bedroom detached house.
Insulation to roof space is 100mm thick in 13m^2 of roof space.
From Part 3.1 - Passive Improvements - Replace and Improve Roof Insulation.
Page 75

		£
Lay 150mm thick glass fibre insulation over existing insulation. Area 13m^2		
10m^2	5m^2 cost £130 = 2 x £130	260
3m^2	3m^2 cost £100	100
		360
Omit contractor's callout charges 2 x £50		-100
(Three charges are included above therefore reduce to one charge)		
Total cost of works		£260
		SAY £280

Example C
Property – 2 bedroom terraced house.
Install solar panels to roof.
From Part 3.1 – Active Improvements - Heating.
Page 103

	£
Installation of panels and connection to existing hot water system.	4,000
Less Grant, from Part 1.5 Page 36	-400
	3,600
Add VAT at 5%	180
(Three charges are included above therefore reduce to one charge)	£3,780
Total cost of works	
	SAY £3,800

1.3 EMPLOYING A CONTRACTOR

When do I use a Contractor?

If you are not a DIY person then you will want to employ a contractor for everything. Even if you are DIY person there are some tasks that it will be prudent to ask a general builder or specialist tradesman to undertake.

Note: Most electrical and all gas work is required to be carried out by a suitably qualified tradesman.

It will always be more economical to 'bundle' work together. If there are several items of repair that need to be done, and you can afford it, then these can be included together in one contract.

When should I consult a Surveyor or Engineer?

For most items of repair and redecorations, contractors can offer all the advice on specification that you will need. However, on larger projects or where there are major structural works, or a high level of design is required, you should consider using the services of a surveyor, engineer or architect.

Finding a Surveyor, Engineer or Architect

There are, again, several ways of finding a local surveyor, architect or engineer although the best method is to contact the various Institutions, such as The Royal Institution of Chartered Surveyors, The Royal Institute of British Architects, and The Institution of Structural Engineers. The details of these organisations can be found in Part Three.

Finding a Contractor

A contractor may be found from a variety of sources:

- Word of mouth from family, friends and neighbours.
- Nameboards outside other properties where work is in progress.
- Contacting the Local Authority.
- Contacting local architects and surveying practices.
- Contacting the Federation of Master Builders to obtain a list of local contractors.
- Advertisements in local newspapers.
- Yellow Pages and Thomsons' telephone directories.
- Internet search.

Selecting a Contractor

It is absolutely essential that you get the right contractor to carry out the work.

Selection of the appropriate contractor/tradesman

Choose a contractor who has experience of doing the type of work that you need doing. If only one type of work is required, then it may be better to select a tradesman, such as a plumber, rather than a general builder.

On specialist items, such as wind turbines, it may be advisable to employ a specialist who installs these on a regular basis.

Choosing a Contractor

You must select the contractor very carefully. While there may be a very large number of local builders, be as selective as possible in order to prevent any future problems, both with the works and finances. The larger the project, the more important this becomes.

In your search for a contractor, BCIS recommends the following sequence:

- Family and friends - obtain recommendations from family and friends in the area, who have had similar work undertaken.
- Recommendation - speak to neighbours to ascertain if a contractor has been recommended by word of mouth.
- Nameboards – when driving around the area, look for nameboards on properties where work is being carried out.
- Local Authority - contact the local planning/building inspection department and ask if they have a list of recommended contractors.
- Local architects/local surveyors - contact them to see if they can recommend any companies.
- Contact the manufacturers of specialist items and ask if they have lists of recommended installers.
- Builders Federations - contact your local builders' association and ask for a list of registered members. The National Federation of Builders has 14 offices around the country, which can provide lists of registered builders in your area. This can similarly be undertaken for specific tradesmen e.g. electricians.

When several names have been collected, contact the companies and ask if you:
- Can inspect current/past work.
- (**Visit** the work, inspect the quality and speak to the owners about the performance and standards of the contractor).
- Obtain references.
- (**Check** the references).
- Does the builder belong to a respected trade body?
- (**Call** the body to confirm membership is current).

Discuss with the contractor/tradesman/ specialist, the work to be undertaken and confirm with them whether and when they will be able to carry out the works.

Where the works are of a substantial nature, the choice of a contractor may be limited to the larger size contractors in the area. Discussions with the contractor and examination of his present and immediate past schemes will reveal his suitability to the works required.

Large contractors sometimes have small works departments who are capable of carrying out minor repairs however, they may charge more as they will have higher overheads (office staff etc) than those of a small builder.

Preparing a Budget for the Works

When putting together a budget for larger projects, it is important that the budget is an estimate of the cost of the work, not an estimate of how much you have to spend.

Once you have prepared a budget for the works, you need to decide if you can afford it. This is particularly important when you are comparing the work involved with the future fuel cost savings and payback period, particularly if you are intending to live in the property for a number of years.

The budget should itemise all the required work and allow a contingency for unforeseen costs. The size of the contingency will depend on how sure you are of what you want and the level of alterations work that may uncover requirements for further work.

A contingency of 5% may be appropriate for a fully designed new extension, while 20% may be more appropriate if you are making major alterations to an old property.

Remember, this is **your** contingency budget, not the builders!

Estimates and Quotations

Before seeking estimates, make sure that you gather together as much information about the work as possible.

Select the appropriate materials. The cheapest are not necessarily the best, especially with regards to duration and future replacement.

Obtain information from manufacturers/installers, as they will advise on the appropriate solution to a problem.

Allow a sum (possibly 10%) for contingency for hidden work or extra work that may arise during the contract. Builders may discover things that need fixing as jobs progress.

Obtain three quotes from contractors/tradesmen including the date that they will be able to commence the work. Ensure that the cost quoted will be fixed to the date they can undertake the work.

Request breakdowns of the quotes to examine and compare prices. A breakdown will also be extremely useful should variations and additional works be needed.

Contracts

A simple contract is a written **offer** to carry out the works for an amount and a written **acceptance** of that offer.

A simple but clear contract should be prepared for small contractors. However, for large contractors, a formal contract using the Joint Contracts Tribunal (JCT) Minor Works Contract may be more appropriate.

Items that should be incorporated into a contract using small contractors/tradesmen should include:

- The cost of the work detailed on the drawing(s)/specification.
- The period of time the work is to be carried out in.

- Client requirements such as the contractor's access to the working area, any limitations on storage of his materials and plant, and any protection required for other areas of the property during the execution of the works.
- The percentage of retention to be held by the client, and at what stage it will be released.
- The payment periods and calculation.
- Space for signature and dating by both parties.

Whilst the JCT contract is far safer both for the client and the contractor, for small builders this may be too onerous and they may be reluctant to price work that includes such a contract. Where the works are of a substantial nature, the employment of a professional surveyor, architect etc, is recommended. They will recommend the form of contract to use and prepare the documentation

Payments

On small contracts, where work may be expected to be completed in a few days, you should agree to pay the contractor on completion. Cash flow is always a problem for small businesses, and builders are no exception, so once you are happy with the work, but only when you are happy, pay promptly.

Never pay in advance. It is almost impossible to recover money overpaid without recourse to expensive legal action. If a contractor asks for payment for materials, agree either to pay the supplier directly or on delivery.

On larger projects, the payment periods and calculation should be specified in the contract.

For example:
'Valuations shall take place on a fortnightly basis and shall be valued on the work completed by that date. Payment shall be made to the contractor within seven days of the valuation.'

Do not pay early for work and especially, do not overpay early.

Include the adjustment for retention with each payment

The calculation of how much is owing to a contractor is called a 'Valuation'.

An example of a valuation is set out as follows:

Value of total scheme including variations	**£23,000**
	£
Valuation No. 2	
Value of work undertaken to date	17,000
Variations No.1 and 2 completed	2,000
Total of work completed	19,000
Less retention @ 5%	950
Total less retention	18,050
Less Valuation 1	10,400
Total	7,650
Value Added Tax @ 17.5%	1,339
Total due to contractor – Valuation No.2	**8,989**

Retention

This is a sum of money set aside by the client [you] from the contract sum until the works are completed to your satisfaction.

The inclusion of retention gives you some financial leverage and safeguard should some items of work, albeit minor, not be completed to your satisfaction. The money withheld will not be released until all the works are completed satisfactorily.

Should the contractor leave the site and not return to complete the outstanding works, you will have funds available to have the work completed by others. You should notify the contractor if you are going to do this.

The details of the retention requirement should be set out in the original contract. It is usual to express retention as a percentage of the cost of the work, 5% being an appropriate and usual percentage.

Any variations should be included in the adjustment for retention.

On completion of the works, carry out an inspection with the contractor and agree where any items have not been finished.

For example:
A new door seal is fitted but the door does not close and on inspection requires planing on one side and subsequently redecorating.

Once the works have been fully completed, the retention can then be released.

As the works progress and payments are made, so the retention should be included with the payment calculations, see example under payments.

Variations and Extras

Always try to avoid changing your mind about what you want. However, even on the best run schemes 'stuff' happens, and changes are required.

Always obtain prices before agreeing for additional works to be undertaken, and confirm the work and cost in writing.

Consult with the contractor as early as possible on possible variations, and ensure variations do not arise on work that has already been completed.

It may be a good idea to include additional works to an existing contract, rather than carry out this work at a later date as a separate job.

For example:
Existing job – improve insulation to loft.

Additional work; construct walkway to water tanks.

When insulation is laid over the existing insulation it is normally laid across the joists and in effect hiding these joists. It will therefore prove difficult to walk across to, for example, water tanks in the loft space as the joists will be hidden from view. A walkway can be constructed to overcome this problem and it will be cheaper and less disruptive to the occupant if this work is undertaken as part of the original contract.

Keep variations and extra work to a minimum. If there are too many variations, or even one variation of large importance/size, then this may have an adverse effect on the contract completion date and therefore could increase costs.

When contracts of repair and refurbishment are undertaken, extra work may arise from hidden unforeseen problems.

For example:
Existing job – replacing windows. On removal of the windows, some lintols are found to have insufficient bearing on the walls and require replacing.

It may be prudent to allow a larger contingency sum in the budget for such works, to cover for any unforeseen or additional works.

1.4 PLANNING AND BUILDING LEGISLATION AND REGULATIONS

Introduction

If you are altering or extending your property there are two kinds of approval that you may require from your local authority.

- Planning permission – this is approval to increase the amount of building, so relates generally to extensions or outbuildings.
- Building Regulations – this is approval that building work is being carried out in accordance with the current Building Regulations. It relates to all new work and all structural alterations.

Planning Permission

Planning permission is the responsibility of the Local Authority.

It is permission to erect or extend a building. At the time of writing, legislation is changing regarding planning permission. Before commencing work therefore, it is recommended that contact should be made with the Local Authority planning officer to seek their requirements and advice. The level of informal advice that you get depends very much on the individual planning officer.

For formal planning permission, the Authority will normally charge a fee. You [the applicant] will be required to submit your application using forms obtainable from the Authority.

Should you do the work without the necessary approvals, the Local Authority can issue an enforcement notice. This notice might require that you seek retrospective planning permission approval. However, there is no guarantee that retrospective permission will be granted. The Local Authority may even require that the completed work be demolished.

Listed buildings and properties in a conservation area have special planning requirements. Similarly, flats also have special planning requirements. It is again recommended that the Local Authority planning officer is consulted as early as possible on these types of properties.

Porches

Planning permission is required for porches if:

- The floor area exceeds 3m².
- Part of the porch is higher than 3m above ground.
- Part of the porch is less than 2m from the boundary between the garden and the public footpath/road.

Replacement windows

Planning permission is required for replacement windows.

Wind turbines

Planning permission is required for wind turbines.

Solar and voltaic panels

Planning permission is required for both types of panels.

Heat pumps

Planning permission is not required for heat pumps as they do not normally involve any visible external works.

Building Regulations

Building Regulations approval is the responsibility of the Local Authority.

These Regulations define how the new building is to be constructed and ensure that the building is structurally safe, and that:

- New or existing foundations are adequate for the new construction.
- Rainwater and drainage conform to requirements.
- Staircases etc meet safety requirements.
- Ventilation, thermal insulation and fire safety regulations are complied with.

It is recommended that, before commencing work on the design, you contact the Local Authority building control officer to seek their requirements and advice.

The Authority will normally charge a fee and the applicant will be required to submit his application using forms obtainable from the Authority. A fee will also be charged for the visits by the building inspector.

The local building inspector will visit the site at specified stages in its construction in order to inspect the work. The building inspector may change requirements following his inspection, if he deems them necessary. For example, one of his

first inspections will be carried out after the foundation trenches have been excavated. He will be in a position to examine the subsoil, and if not of a requisite standard, he could instruct that the depth of foundation be increased before the concrete is poured.

Cavity Wall insulation

Building Regulations approval is required. If you use an approved installer they will generally submit a Building Notice on your behalf as a matter of course.

Porches

Building Regulations approval is required:
- When floor area exceeds 30m².

Wind turbines

Building Regulations approval and planning permission is required for wind turbines.

Solar and voltaic panels

Building Regulations approval may be required for both types of panels.

Heat pumps

Building Regulations approval may be required for heat pumps. This will depend on how the system is linked to the existing heating/hot water system.

All electrical work

Part P (Electrical Safety) of the Building Regulations now requires all electrical work to be carried out by certified people, except very limited work.

Work that can be carried out by **non-certified** operatives:
- Replacement of light fittings, sockets, switches.
- Replacement of damaged cable for a single circuit.
- Work not in the bathroom and kitchen comprising;
- Additional lighting, fittings and switches to existing circuit.
- Additional sockets and fused spurs to existing ring or radial main.
- Additional earth bonding.

These works are conditional upon:
- The use of suitable cable and fittings for the particular application.
- Circuit protective measures are unaffected and suitable for protecting the new circuit.
- All works comply with all other appropriate regulations.

Work that must be carried out by **certified** operatives:
- All new modifications to electrical wiring within bathrooms and shower rooms.
- Installation or modification to underfloor heating.
- Installation or modification to ceiling heating.
- Power or lighting to garden.
- Specialist installations.

DIY work
Building Regulations will apply equally to DIY work and work undertaken by a contractor. The Local Authority will need to be notified of DIY changes before the work is commenced. The work will be inspected and tested.

Certificates
You will need to keep the appropriate certificates from the Local Authority to prove that any work was approved. You will need to produce them when you come to sell the house.

Party Walls
If the property is a terraced or semi detached house then a wall (or walls if a mid terrace) will be shared with a neighbour. This shared wall is known as the party wall.

In some cases, if excavations or constructing foundations for a new construction are within 3m or 6m of the neighbouring property, then written consent will be required.

Similarly, if a wind turbine is required to be attached to a party wall, a shared chimney stack for example, then written consent will also be required

Your neighbour cannot in normal circumstances withhold consent, as long as the provisions of the Party Wall etc Act are followed.

The Party Wall etc. Act 1996
The Party Wall etc. Act 1996 produced a procedure for homeowners in England and Wales. It applies to all building work involving a party wall or party fence wall. The Act was designed to minimise disputes by ensuring property owners use a surveyor to determine the time and way in which the work is carried out.

An 'agreed surveyor' can be used to act for both owners should problems arise.

The Act covers the following and written agreement is required:

- Bearing of beam – cutting into wall for e.g. a loft conversion or supporting upper floor after removal of a loadbearing internal wall.
- Damp proof course – inserting new all the way through the wall.
- Underpinning the party wall.
- Demolishing and rebuilding the party wall.
- Raising the whole party wall including cutting off any objects, if necessary preventing this from happening.
- Protecting adjoining walls by cutting a flashing into an adjoining building.
- Building a new wall on the line of the junction between two properties.
- Excavating foundations:
  - Within 3m of an adjoining structure and lower than its foundation.
  - Within 6m of an adjoining structure and below a line drawn down 45 degrees from the bottom of its foundation.

The Act does not cover the following and written agreement is not required:

- Minor works not affecting your neighbour's part of the party wall.
  - Fixing plugs.
  - Fixing skirting or other woodwork.
  - Screwing in wall units.
  - Screwing in shelving.
  - Replastering walls.
  - Adding or replacing electrical wiring or socket outlet.

Notice of party wall work
Written notice must be given to neighbours:
- **At least two months** before starting any party wall works.
- **One month** for building a wall between properties or excavation works.

If tenants or leaseholders live next door, the landlord must also be informed. Written notice must also be given to owners living above or below the property.

Endeavour to talk to neighbours before issuing notices as this can prevent any future problems.

Neighbours should give written approval within 14 days of receipt of the notice.

Disputes
If there is a dispute:
- Both parties appoint their own surveyor, or
- Both parties appoint an 'agreed surveyor'.

The surveyor will draw up the 'Award', a document that details work to be carried out, when and how it is to be done, and a record of the condition of the adjoining property before the work is started.

The Award will determine who will pay for the work if this is in dispute, although this is generally the property owner who started the work.

Party wall guidance
A useful guide, 'Party Wall Guidance' can be obtained free of charge from the Royal Institution of Chartered Surveyors. It provides information on party wall law and where you can go for advice. Visit: www.rics.org/partywalls.

Building Materials
The selection of building materials will be dependent upon the existing property, especially the external fabric. Another factor is how close it is to other buildings and how they are constructed. These factors affect the materials and design, particularly the front elevation/ elevation facing the main road.

Building materials do have a bearing, both when obtaining Planning and Building Regulations approval. It is again recommended that you discuss selection before going ahead.

Where possible, and especially on the elevation facing the main road, the materials chosen for the external fabric such as bricks, roof tiles, windows, doors, should match or be sympathetic with the existing property.

1.5 GRANTS AND VAT

Grants

At the time of writing, there are a number of grants available to householders, some of which are listed below. They are obtained from Local Authorities and the organisations below, and the householder is therefore recommended to contact them to discuss whether the work they envisage qualifies for a grant, what proportion of the cost may be given by the Authority, and the rules governing the award of a grant.

The law sets out a framework of all the various work that is eligible for a grant, however, each authority may have their particular guidelines to determine what work has funding priority.

In England and Wales, grants are available under the Low Carbon Buildings Programme from the Department for Business, Enterprise and Regulatory Reform (BERR), (website: www.lowcarbonbuildings.org. uk/home) for solar panels, photovoltaic panels and wind pumps. There is a £2500 grant cap per household

In Scotland, grants under the Scottish Community and Householder Renewables Initiative (SCHRI) are available for solar panels and wind pumps only (website: www. energysavingtrust.org.uk/schri/) Applications can also be made for separate grants for two different technologies.

In Northern Ireland, grants are available from Reconnect, which is administered by Action Renewables (website: www.reconnect.org.uk/).

The Landlord's Energy Saving Allowance

The Landlord's Energy Savings Allowance (LESA) allows the costs of acquiring and installing energy-saving items in residential rented properties to be deducted from profits. The allowance can be claimed for all expenditure on loft, solid wall, cavity wall and floor insulation, draught proofing and hot water system insulation. The annual allowance is £1,500 per property, rather than per building as was previously the case, and the LESA will be available for qualifying expenditure up to 2015.

The LESA was introduced in the Finance Act 2004 but was restricted to residential landlords. The extension to include corporate landlords was announced in the 2006 Pre Budget Report and legislated in the 2007 Finance Act. As the extension constitutes a state aid, it could only be activated, as it now has been, once formally approved by the European Commission. The allowance will be available on all expenditure incurred on or after 8 July 2008.

Those wishing to take advantage of this allowance are advised to consult their professional advisors.

Solar Panels

England and Wales: a maximum of £400 or 30% of the relevant eligible costs, whichever is the lower.

Scotland: the grant is 30% of installation costs up to £4000.

Northern Ireland: the grant for installation is £1125 regardless of size but subject to an overall 50% limit of installed costs, inclusive of VAT.

Photovoltaic panels.

England and Wales: a maximum of £2000 per KWp installed, and with an overall maximum grant of £2500 or 50% of the relevant eligible costs, whichever is the lower.

Scotland: at present, no grants are available.

Northern Ireland: the grant for installation is £3000 per KWp up to £15000 maximum and subject to an overall 50% limit of installed costs, inclusive of VAT.

WindTurbines

England and Wales: a maximum of £1000 per KWp installed, and with an overall maximum grant of £2500 or 30% of the relevant eligible costs, whichever is the lower.

Scotland: the grant is 30% of installation costs up to £4000.

Northern Ireland: the grant for installation is £2000 per KWp up to £8000 maximum and subject to an overall 50% limit of installed costs, inclusive of VAT.

Ground or Water Source Heat Pumps

England and Wales: a maximum of £1200 or 30% of the relevant eligible costs, whichever is the lower.

Scotland: the grant is 30% of installation costs up to £4000, including all ground works.

Northern Ireland: the grant for installation is £3000 regardless of size, subject to an overall 40% limit of installed costs, inclusive of VAT. The air source heat pump's grant for installation is £2400 regardless of size, subject to an overall 40% limit of installed costs, inclusive of VAT

Small hydro

England and Wales: a maximum of £1000 per KW of installed capacity subject to an overall maximum grant of £2500 or 30% of the relevant eligible costs, whichever is the lower.

Scotland: the grant is 30% of installation costs up to £4000 including all ground works.

Northern Ireland: the grant for installation is £2000 up to a maximum grant of £8000, regardless of size, subject to an overall 50% limit of installed costs, inclusive of VAT.

Biomass stoves

England and Wales: a maximum of £600 or 20% of the relevant eligible costs, whichever is the lower.

Scotland: the grant is 30% of installation costs up to £4000 including all ground works.

Northern Ireland: the grant for installation is £1500 regardless of size, subject to an overall 50% limit of installed costs, inclusive of VAT.

Biomass boilers

England and Wales: a maximum of £1500 or 20% of the relevant eligible costs, whichever is the lower.

Scotland: the grant is 30% of installation costs up to £4000 including all ground works.

Northern Ireland: the grant for installation is £32500 regardless of size, subject to an overall 50% limit of installed costs, inclusive of VAT.

Insulation

These may be available to cover the cost of works to improve the thermal insulation of a property. Current information can be obtained from the Energy Efficiency Advice Centre (telephone 0800 512012).

Energy Saving Trust

The Energy Saving Trust has a website which provides information on the types of grant available, www.energysavingtrust.org.uk.

VAT

At the time of writing, there is a reduced rate of 5% for the installation of energy saving materials. This relates to the supply and installation of the products. The reduction will not be applicable if the materials are only supplied and not installed.

Items subject to the reduced levy are:

Central heating and hot water system controls
Draught stripping
Insulation
Solar panels
Photovoltaic panels
Wind turbines
Ground and air source heat pumps.

PART TWO

2.1 INTRODUCTION

ENERGY IMPROVEMENT PRODUCTS

There are varied ways of improving the home energy efficiency of a dwelling and its garden. These have been listed and detailed below under the following headings:

Passive improvements

This covers improving the insulation levels of a property. This includes roof spaces, external walls, windows and doors, ground floor and pipework. In general, items in this section do not include machinery and require little or no maintenance once installed.

Replacement of existing equipment

Replacement of items normally found in houses such as boilers, water heaters, metering equipment and appliances with energy efficient alternatives are covered here. In general, items in this section include machinery that requires maintenance once installed.

Active improvements

This section provides prices for the installation of solar panels, voltaic panels, heat pumps, and wind turbines. This section deals with the use of rainwater to provide irrigation for gardens, and grey water systems for houses. These items involve the installation of new plant and machinery and have maintenance and service life considerations.

Insulation

Insulation can provide the simplest way of saving energy in a home, particularly in older houses. This can include insulation to external walls, to ground, floors, to lofts in pitched roofs or to flat roofs; the installation of secondary double glazing, new replacement double or triple glazing to windows and external doors, and installing draught proofing around external and internal door frames.

External Walls

Providing insulation to external walls can be undertaken in several ways and will be dependent upon the wall structure.

For cavity wall construction, the cavity can be injected through holes of 22 to 25mm diameter made in the outside skin of the wall and made good after completion of the works. The most common injection forms are u.f.foam (urea formaldehyde foam) and e.p.s. beads (polystyrene beads combined with a building agent or adhesive at the time of injection). This work should be carried out by a specialist contractor.

For older properties, constructed with solid walls and rendered externally, the rendering can be removed, and a rigid insulation board fixed to the external face. Metal lathing is then fixed to the board and the face re-rendered as before. You may be able to insulate and render a brick house externally but you should check with your local authority planning department. For all solid walls, insulation board can be fixed to the inside face of the wall by removing the existing plaster, installing the board and replastering. These works can be undertaken by a general builder.

Diagram 1:

External Cavity Wall: Cavity wall injection

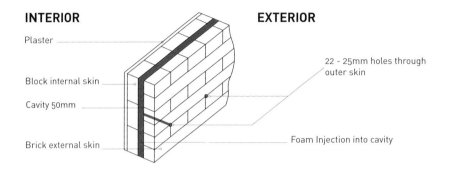

INTERIOR

EXTERIOR

Plaster

Block internal skin

Cavity 50mm

Brick external skin

22 - 25mm holes through outer skin

Foam Injection into cavity

External Solid Wall: Insulation board to external face of wall

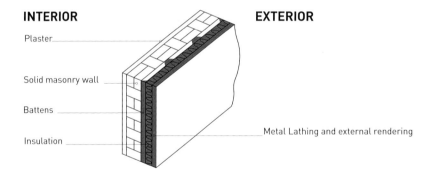

INTERIOR

EXTERIOR

Plaster

Solid masonry wall

Battens

Insulation

Metal Lathing and external rendering

External Solid Wall: Insulation board to interior face of wall

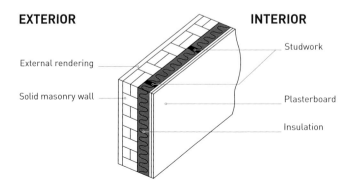

EXTERIOR

INTERIOR

External rendering

Solid masonry wall

Studwork

Plasterboard

Insulation

Roofs

The greatest heat loss is through the roof and as much as 20% of the energy bill can be saved by installing insulation. Simple works can be carried out to reduce this loss in pitched roofs, although insulating flat roofs can prove more difficult.

Loft spaces to pitched roofs can be insulated with mineral wool quilt, blown mineral wool or blown cellular fibre. The roof space should have the following thicknesses to provide the best insulation; glass wool 270mm, rockwool 250mm, cellulose 220mm.

Should existing insulation in the loft be 100 or 150mm thick, then this should be topped up to the recommended thicknesses. This can be undertaken by laying the new insulation across the ceiling joists rather than between them. However if the insulation is laid in this way, then a walkway across the joists to equipment in the roof, such as water tanks, is recommended.

Insulation should never be laid under water tanks in the loft or around pipework in case a leakage of water occurs in the equipment. Similarly, electrical cabling should be laid over insulation and, where ceiling downlighters are installed, they should have proprietary protective boxing.

An alternative to using insulation quilt to increase the insulation in a roof space where the roof space is boarded for storage, or requires boarding for storage, is to lay and fix rigid insulation over the ceiling joists. The boarding can then be laid over this insulation.

Insulation to flat roofs is more difficult as there is no easy access to the structure. When a flat roof covering is due for replacement, normally 15 to 20 years after initial installation, this will be the most efficient and cost effective method of installing insulation. The works can be undertaken by either a specialist installer or a general builder. Rigid foam boards will be laid to the existing roof structure with the new felt roofing covering as before.

Diagram 2:
Loft: No insulation

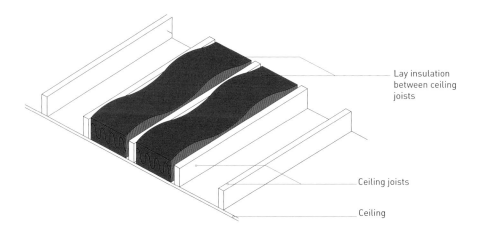

Lay insulation
between ceiling
joists

Ceiling joists

Ceiling

Loft: Insufficient insulation

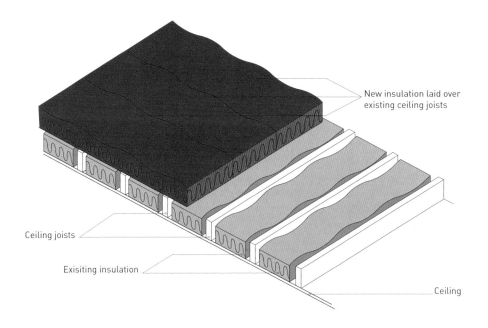

New insulation laid over
existing ceiling joists

Ceiling joists

Exisiting insulation

Ceiling

Floors

Suspended timber floors are a construction comprising floorboards fixed to joists on small brick walls that have been built off the concrete slab. The laying of a good quality underlay and carpet will assist in reducing heat loss. The floor can also be insulated by lifting the floorboards and laying mineral wool insulation that is supported by netting between the joists.

Gaps between floorboards and skirtings can be sealed by using a regular tube sealant, e.g. silicon sealant.

The airbricks in an external wall should not be filled in to prevent draughts. Air bricks provide a means of ventilation to the timber joists, thereby preventing rotting of the joists to the suspended floor.

Solid floors can also be insulated by the removal of the existing screed, the laying of insulation boards on top of the site slab, then screed being laid on top of the insulation. In existing properties, this will create further cost increases as the floor height will be raised by 100mm as a result. Skirtings, chimney hearths, door openings and possibly central heating pipework and radiators, will require adjustment, which will add considerably to both the disruption and cost. The most cost effective method of inserting insulation to a solid floor is when undertaking major refurbishment or alteration work to a property. When constructing a new extension, laying insulation to the floor is now a Building Regulations' requirement.

Diagram 3(a): Suspended timber floor

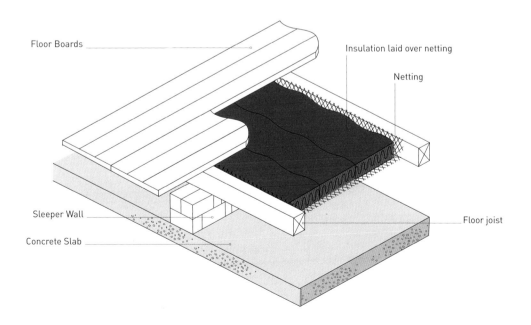

Floor Boards

Insulation laid over netting

Netting

Sleeper Wall

Floor joist

Concrete Slab

Diagram 3(b): Solid concrete floor

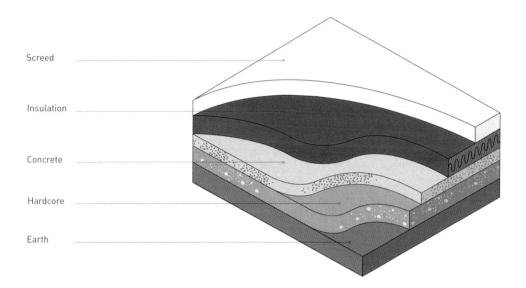

Screed

Insulation

Concrete

Hardcore

Earth

Windows

Windows cause one of the greatest heat losses from a building, although they can assist in solar heat gain especially on south facing elevations. On older windows, where the glazing is unique or difficult to reproduce by modern methods, secondary glazing can be installed to improve the thermal performance. The secondary glazing should have means of opening, both for ventilation and fire safety needs.

The most common way of improving thermal performance is by replacing the existing windows with sealed double or triple glazed units. Planning permission is now required when replacing windows to a property but there is a significant variety of units available today which will enable the property's character to be maintained.

Sash and casement windows can be replaced with both uPVC and timber units.

Where the window frame has rotted, it may be more beneficial to resources if the frame can be easily repaired, especially if the window is double glazed. The damaged area, e.g. part of a window sill, can be cut out and a new piece of timber spliced in. This will save on the energy costs of producing a new window, transportation, fitting and the disposal of the old window.

Cracking may occur around window frames when an opening casement has been regularly slammed because it has been sticking. The cracks can be repaired by applying a silicone sealant. Repairing the opening casement should also be undertaken in order to ease the movement.

Doors

Glazed external doors suffer similar problems to windows and again replacement double glazed doors are now readily available.

Rotten door frames could be repaired rather than totally replaced.

Cracks that have occurred around door frames can be sealed using a silicone sealant. These may have resulted from sticking doors that have been constantly slammed shut. Repairing the door should also be undertaken to ease the closing and therefore eliminate any future cracking.

Repairs to internal doors to ensure they fit correctly, help to eliminate draughts. Draught proofing around internal doors is also a way of retaining heat to rooms, especially those that require a higher temperature, e.g. lounges. This is effective yet inexpensive and enables draughts to be eliminated and comfort levels to be maintained.

Other Works

Conservatories and sun lounges
Passive solar heat gain can be achieved by constructing conservatories, sun lounges, garden rooms etc on the south facing elevation of a property. This structure can act as both a heat store and provides additional insulation. The internal wall will become a store for heat that will radiate back out after sunset.

Porches
These structures provide additional insulation for front or side entrances to a property, particularly if north facing. They can be of proprietary construction or purpose built to suit the appearance of the existing dwelling.

Rooflights
These can be installed in properties such as chalet bungalows where natural lighting in an area such as a hall and landing is poor and electric lighting is required. Rooflights can increase the natural lighting to the area thereby saving the need for artificial lighting.

Diagram 4(a): Chalet Bungalow Rooflight

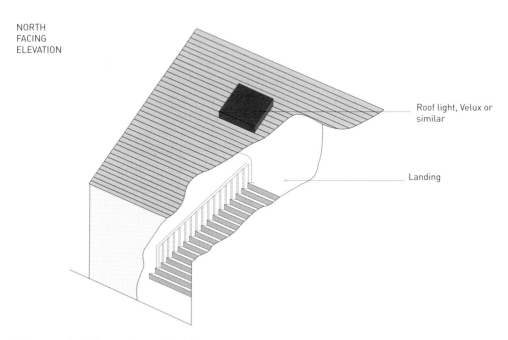

NORTH
FACING
ELEVATION

Roof light, Velux or
similar

Landing

Diagram 4(b): Bungalow Rooflight

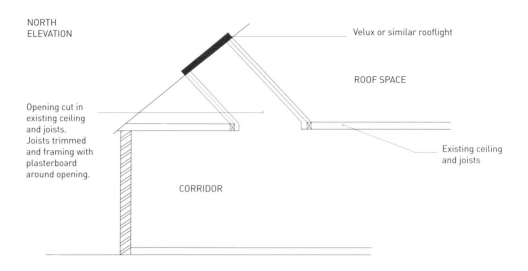

NORTH
ELEVATION

Velux or similar rooflight

ROOF SPACE

Opening cut in
existing ceiling
and joists.
Joists trimmed
and framing with
plasterboard
around opening.

Existing ceiling
and joists

CORRIDOR

2.3 REPLACEMENT OF EXISTING EQUIPMENT

Heating

Boilers
Boilers should be sized correctly for each type of house and should take account of any improvements that have been made to the property since the previous boiler was installed. This will include extensions and improvements to the insulation. Oversizing of boilers will result in higher heating bills and CO_2 emissions as the boiler will run less efficiently.

The Energy Saving Trust web site has more information on boilers. The SEDBUK (Seasonal Efficiency of Domestic Boilers in the UK) web site at www.sedbuk.com calculates how efficient your existing gas or oil boiler is. The rating represents the average annual efficiency. It also lists the most current and obsolete boilers.

Central heating systems should be maintained regularly in order to maintain their efficiency. Boilers should be serviced regularly in accordance with the manufacturers/installers recommendations. Pipework should be flushed out with chemical additives to break up any build up of sludge deposits. An inhibitor can be added to the water at the time of installation, to prevent this build up occurring. This should be checked from time to time especially if radiators have been added to the system or there has been a leak.

Radiators
Radiators should be situated near or under windows.

Radiator foil should also be used, affixed to the wall behind the radiator to reflect the heat back into the room rather than through the structure, thereby saving energy costs.

Thermostatic radiator valves (TRV's) set the temperature in each room. These are therefore more efficient than a wall thermostat as this is either positioned in the hall or lounge and will not allow for required changes in temperature in other rooms. TRV's can set the temperature in each room at a different level. TRV's are now standard on new installations but they can be easily fitted to radiators, replacing the existing valves. Whilst new slimline radiators are more efficient than traditional radiators, the existing radiators, when removed, will need to be dumped, which will adversely affect the environment.

When TRV's are fitted to all the existing radiators, an automatic bypass valve will need to be fitted at the boiler, by a plumber.

Biomass
Biomass, bioenergy or biofuels are produced from organic materials. This can either be from plants or from industrial, commercial, agricultural or domestic products. They do not include fossil fuels, which have taken millions of years to develop.

There are two types of Biomass products:
Woody - products from forests, untreated wood products, energy crops and short rotation coppice (e.g willow).

Non woody - animal waste, industrial / biodegradable municipal products from food processing/high energy crops (e.g. sugar cane).

Biomass can be used to heat homes by either a stand alone stove or boiler. The fuel used can be logs, wood pellets or wood chips. Access to a local supplier will be imperative and a suitable storage space will be required for either of these systems. The vent must be designed for these appliances and the installation must comply with Building Regulations and Planning Regulations if the building is in a protected area of outstanding beauty. Existing chimneys can be utilised by fitting a lining to the flue.

Logs, depending upon the quality and quantity, cost between £20/m³ to £60/m³. The quantity will be dependent upon the amount of space the householder has to store the wood.

Wood pellets can cost between £140/tonne to £200/tonne depending upon the method of delivery and location. They can either be delivered in bags on pallets, or blown through tubes or pipes to a suitable storage area.

The cost of wood chips can range between £45/tonne to £67/tonne. This again will be dependant upon the quantity required and location. Delivery is made straight off the back of a lorry into a suitable store, therefore the user will need to consider if there is sufficient access to be able to do this. The quantity will again be dependent upon the amount of storage space available and the householder will also need to consider accessibility for the delivery of the chips.

The cost per kW/hr for wood chips ranges from 1.6p to 2.5p and for wood pellets from 3p to 3.5p. This compares very favourably with fuel oil and gas, which range from 2.4p to 8p and upwards.

Stand alone stoves
These provide heating to a room. Some can provide water and central heating if they are fitted with a back boiler. They are about 80% efficient and are normally used for background heating, and as a feature in a room.

Boilers
These provide hot water and central heating to a house. Boilers using logs are loaded by hand, whereas boilers using wood pellets or wood chips can be loaded automatically. These boilers are usually larger in size than gas or oil boilers. Their capacity will range from 5 to 60Kw depending upon the size of the property, and it can meet all hot water and space heating requirements.

Fuel cell boiler
This is a new innovation whereby domestic boilers produce electricity as well as heat. These boilers, powered by fuel cells, generate heat and electricity when fuel, natural gas, is passed across the surface of the cells.

The cells comprise a cube of cells, each approximately the size of a compact disc case but wafer thin.

Plumbing and Services

Hot Water Pipes and Cylinders

Heat can be lost along the whole length of hot water pipes especially those in the coldest places, e.g. the loft. The pipes which are nearest to the hot water cylinder will be the hottest and consequently will lose heat the quickest.

Cold Water Pipes and Tanks

It is similarly imperative to insulate cold water pipes, especially in cold areas such as lofts. This is to prevent water freezing in the pipes and the pipes/joints cracking as a result, causing water leakage. The cold water storage tanks should also be suitably insulated, particularly as they are normally sited in the coldest part of the house, e.g. the loft.

The water main from the Water Company stopcock to the internal stopcock is the responsibility of the householder. Where there is a water leak in this pipework, this should be repaired to prevent wastage.

Electrical

Light bulbs

Low energy light bulbs, whilst at present more expensive than traditional bulbs, have one of the fastest payback times as they use up to a quarter of the energy required by traditional bulbs. Less heat is generated from these low energy bulbs and therefore most of the energy produces light rather than heat.

Appliances

Electrical appliances that display the Energy Efficiency Recommended logo meet or exceed government-approved energy efficiency requirements.

Appliances can be compared with one another, as each appliance will carry an EU Energy Efficiency Label. Most appliances are rated on a scale of A to G, with A being the most efficient, although refrigeration products now go up to A++. Retailers and manufacturers must display these labels on all new domestic appliances. Buying a more efficient model will not mean you're losing out on performance, but it will mean it will be cheaper to run and therefore more environmentally friendly.

Laundry and dishwashing labels also have similar ratings for washing, spin and/or drying performance, with A rating again being the best. Further significant electricity savings can be made if a washing machine is operated using a 30°C cycle rather than a 40°C or 60°C wash cycle.

Dishwashers, on average, complete around 250 cycles and by using an energy efficient model savings of approximately £15 per year could be made on the electricity bill, together with smaller savings on water bills. Similarly, the purchase of a new Energy Efficiency Recommended fridge-freezer could save you up to £35 a year on your electricity bill, and help reduce your carbon dioxide output.

Smart Metering

A Smart Meter is an advanced meter which can be used for electricity, gas or water metering. It can identify the consumption in more detail than a conventional meter and can transmit that information, via a network, back to the local utility for both monitoring and billing purposes.

Traditional meters measure total consumption use by the household. They provide no information on when the energy was used. Smart meters measure both the consumption and when the energy was used by the household. They therefore allow price setting agencies to introduce different prices for consumption based on the time of day and the season.

The use of electricity, gas and water varies during the day and season. It peaks at certain predictable times and if generation is constrained, prices can rise significantly during these times. These rises can be caused by the purchase of more expensive sources of fuel or by bringing more costly generation online.

The householder will then be billed both by consumption and the time of day, allowing the householder to adjust some usage to times when the cost will be considerably cheaper. For example, using washing machines and dishwashers at night when the cost is cheapest.

The data produced by this monitoring method will ensure all energy bills are accurate; future bills can be forecast allowing for energy budgeting.

2.4 ACTIVE IMPROVEMENTS

Heating

Solar panels
Solar panels collect the sun's energy and convert it to heat water.

There are, at present, two types available; flat plate and evacuated tube. As evacuated tube panels are more efficient, smaller panels can be used for the same output. They are, however, more expensive than flat plate collectors but can be used on more limited roof areas.

These units can also be installed on the face of the dwelling, or even on the ground, as long as there are no obstructions to the sun during the warm parts of the day.

Liquid, which is water mixed with antifreeze, is heated in the pipes in the panel and then pumped into the coil in the indirect cylinder, where water is pumped from the mains then heated by the coil. This system can be used in conjunction with the existing heat source. Water will be heated by the boiler and taken into a separate coil to supplement the panel's heating.

Diagram 5: Solar panels

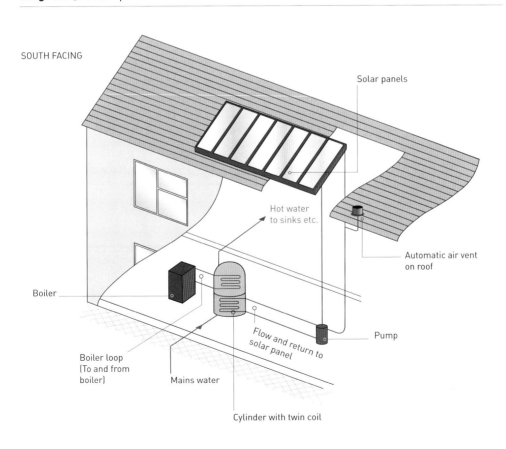

SOUTH FACING

Solar panels

Hot water to sinks etc.

Automatic air vent on roof

Boiler

Pump

Boiler loop (To and from boiler)

Mains water

Flow and return to solar panel

Cylinder with twin coil

Heat pumps

Heat pump systems can be used to provide either heating or cooling. These systems can, depending on type, extract heat from or send excess heat to, a reservoir such as the air, the ground or a body of water. Domestic fridges are actually heat pumps and work by using the physical properties of a liquid or gas refrigerant, circulated by a pump to transfer heat from the inside to the outside of the fridge. You will notice that when your fridge is working, the coil at the back of the unit gets quite hot and this is energy that has been extracted from the inside of the fridge by the heat pump. Air conditioning units use exactly the same principle.

Heat pump systems can be very efficient because the amount of heating they can deliver is greater than the energy used by the pump circulating the fluid. The machine is configured to maintain a temperature difference between the circulating fluid and the reservoir. In this case, a reservoir is anything which can either have its heat extracted for use in the building or can take waste heat away. The reservoir may be the air, the ground or a body of water.

Ground source pumps – this is a form of solar energy used for space and water heating. It is best used with underfloor heating systems as they run at lower water temperature than conventional radiator systems.

The ground is heated by the sun and the low grade energy from the ground is converted on the same principle as a refrigerator, only in reverse, to a usable energy at higher temperature.

This system uses the groundwater in either an open or closed loop system and pumps it to the surface where the heat energy is extracted by a heat pump and the water is returned to the ground. The heat pumps require energy to run them but this will be exceeded by the energy gained.

The main components comprise a compressor, expansion valve and two heat exchangers. These are connected and refrigerant is driven through the closed circuit by the pump.

They are appropriate for new build or where there is a substantial area of ground, or where the drilling of a deep hole is possible. It can also be advantageous if there is no available mains gas supply.

The added advantage is that in summer, some systems can be reversed to take the heat out of the building and deposit it in the ground. Cooling and air conditioning can therefore be provided.

There is no requirement for an annual safety inspection. The circulation pumps are unlikely to be guaranteed for more than one year. The compressor is likely to be guaranteed for up to three years and to have a life of up to 15 years.

Air-source pumps – these operate on the same principle as ground source pumps but they are cheaper to install. However, in cold weather the air will be at a much lower temperature and the system's efficiency will drop, as the pump will need to work harder to supply the heat required. They can be used in conjunction with another heating source and the pump will then only operate when it is at its most efficient.

Water-source pumps – heat is collected in the same way as the ground source system, through an open or closed loop system, but from nearby bodies of water. If rivers or public bodies of water are used, then permission must be sought from the Environment Agency.

Diagram 6: Ground source heat pumps (open loop system)

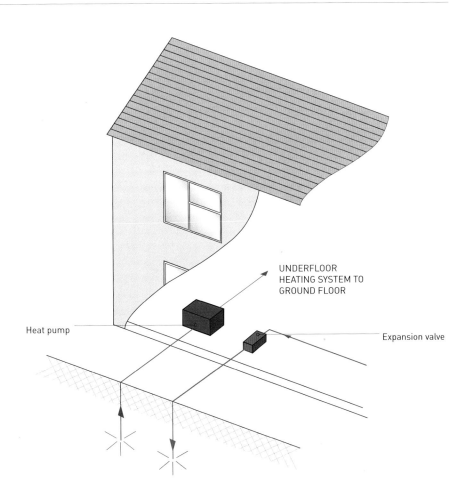

UNDERFLOOR HEATING SYSTEM TO GROUND FLOOR

Heat pump

Expansion valve

Power

Photovoltaic panels

Photovoltaic panels comprise cells which convert the energy in light into electrical energy. They are grouped into modules with one panel containing several modules. The panels do not require direct sunlight and generate power in cloudy conditions.

The panels are situated on south facing, 30° to 40° pitched roofs with no overshading from trees or adjacent buildings. The panels can also be installed on flat roofs but they will require angled mounting brackets. The roof should be checked to ensure that it can support the structure. The panels require very little maintenance but they should be cleaned to maintain optimum light transmission. The regularity will be dependent upon the location of the property. A house near a busy main road or within close proximity of trees, will require more regular cleaning than one in a quiet rural area not surrounded by trees.

Direct current is produced at a low voltage and an inverter then converts the power into 240V alternating current. The panels are connected to the inverter by cables and this is then connected to the mains.

Roof tile cells are now available. These are more expensive but can be more cost effective if reroofing a dwelling or building a new property.

Diagram 7: Photovoltaic Panels

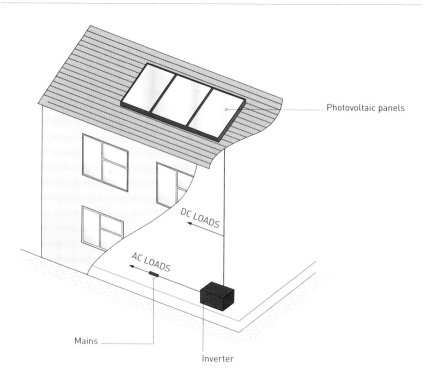

Photovoltaic panels

DC LOADS

AC LOADS

Mains

Inverter

Wind turbines

Wind turbines harness the wind to produce electrical power. There are two basic types of wind turbine:

Mini wind turbines, which are building mounted, and small wind turbines which are pole mounted on the ground and independent from the building.

A built in circuit breaker or a fused connection unit switch on the incoming supply is required to limit the speed and the power generated by the turbine.

Maintenance is low on wind turbines with a service check required every few years.

Diagram 8: Wind Turbine

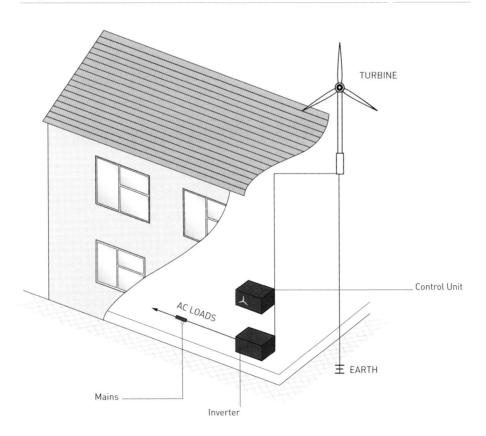

Combined Heating and Power

Photovoltaic and solar roof tiles

Roof tiles are now available which perform the same function as photovoltaic and solar panels. They can either be used on new build or when an existing dwelling is to be reroofed. Planning permission is usually not required as they do not alter the roof line. In conservation areas, however, the planning officer should be contacted and the proposals discussed with him.

One photovoltaic or solar tile is the equivalent in area of four traditional roof tiles, and they are attached straight to the roof battens by the roofing contractor.

Photovoltaic and solar roof tiles can be laid together on a roof, thereby providing both solar electricity and heated water to a property.

Microchip combined heat and power

This system takes the heat from a gas or oil filled engine which drives a generator producing power. The heat, which would normally be lost, is absorbed through coolant water in a high efficiency heat exchanger.

1Kw of power creates 2Kw of usable heat energy.

The energy stored as hot water is then used for either central heating (directly) or air conditioning (indirectly).

Ventilation, Heat Recovery and Comfort Cooling

In well insulated homes, particularly modern properties with double glazing and central heating, air pollution can become very bad.

Extractor fans are fitted to wet areas such as kitchens, utility rooms, bathrooms and cloakrooms and trickle vents may be fitted in all windows to allow air to return into the dwelling. These, however, will no longer be required if a Heat Recovery System is installed into a dwelling.

Heat Recovery systems are designed to change all the air in the dwelling at least once every two hours. The stale damp air is thereby replaced with fresh, clean, filtered and warmed air. Recovery Ventilation systems recover heat lost through the trickle vents and other 'gaps' in the dwelling.

The Heat Recovery Unit can be located in the roof space, above a cooker hood, at high level in a cupboard, or wall mounted. A ducting system connects the stale air exhaust grille to the Recovery Unit and extracts the stale air via ducting to all the wet areas. Fresh air passes through the heat exchanger, picking up the heat recovered from the stale air. The warmed fresh air is then ducted to all the habitable rooms.

A Comfort Cooling unit can be fitted with this system. The unit will cool and dehumidify the supply air by between 8° and 12° centigrade on the outside temperature. This results in a 2° to 3° centigrade temperature drop within a room, although this reduction will vary depending upon the amount of heat gain within the building and the amount of air provided by the ventilation system.

A filter can also be installed which can remove pollen, bacteria, smoke, traffic fumes and viruses.

Rainwater Harvesting and Greywater

Rainwater butts
Butts can be installed to fill directly from the downpipes from roof gutters. The water is diverted from the downpipe by means of a diverter and overflow, which will ensure that the butt does not overflow.
The butt should be mounted on a brick base or similar, in order that a watering can may be placed under the tap.

The rainwater can be further utilised to irrigate gardens by the use of land drains, a series of porous pipes laid in a gravel surround.

Storage tanks
Tanks are sited above or below ground and collect water from the roof gutters. This water is used for toilets and washing machines.

A tank situated above ground will require insulating to protect from freezing in winter. A filtration system will be required to prevent leaves etc from entering the tank. When the tank is full, further rainwater will drain off into the normal drainage system. Float switches should be installed in the tank so that when the water level drops to a

minimum level, the mains water feed can be opened to partly fill the tank. The collected water can be pumped to a separate header tank, which would be situated in the loft. The water could be pumped directly to the fittings, although should the pump fail, the toilet would require flushing with a bucket of water.

Greywater systems
This water is again used for flushing toilets. It is water that is recovered from a property's baths, showers and basins.

This water is stored in underground tanks outside the building.

This system requires a settlement tank and filtration treatment to remove all contaminants. The system also requires disinfectant and biological cleansing to remove organic compounds. When full, the overflow can drain off water from the tank into the normal drainage system. The tank should also be emptied when the water has been stored for a long period of time.

Diagram 9(a): Rainwater Harvesting

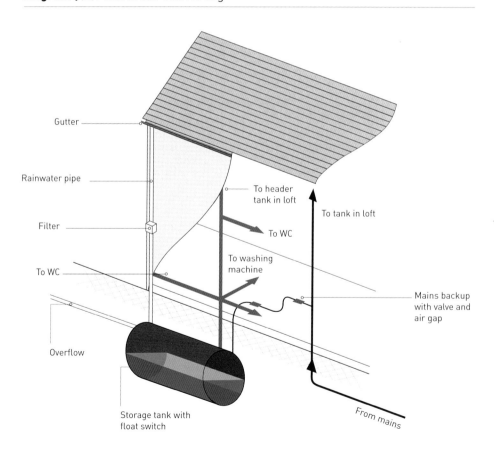

Gutter

Rainwater pipe

Filter

To WC

Overflow

Storage tank with
float switch

To header
tank in loft

To tank in loft

To WC

To washing
machine

Mains backup
with valve and
air gap

From mains

Diagram 9(b): Greywater Recycling System

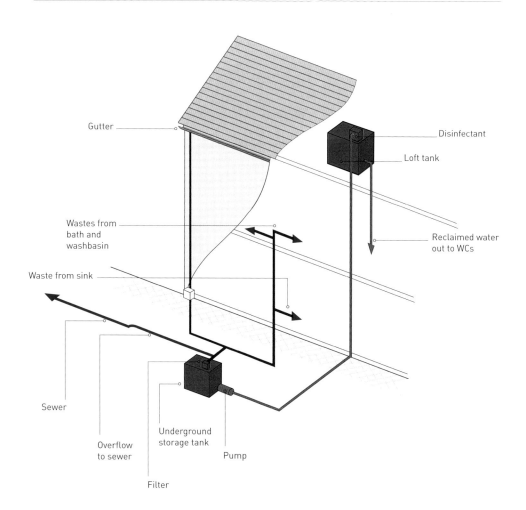

Gutter

Disinfectant

Loft tank

Wastes from
bath and
washbasin

Reclaimed water
out to WCs

Waste from sink

Sewer

Overflow
to sewer

Underground
storage tank

Pump

Filter

Micro grey water systems

Micro greywater recycling systems can now be installed into domestic properties. The system recycles water from WCs, showers and baths and comprises a cleaning tank where a skimmer removes surface debris such as foam, hair and soap. The heavier waste particles sink to the bottom and are flushed away to the waste pipe. The remaining 'clean' water is then transferred to a 100litre capacity storage tank for use in toilet flushing. The unit is housed in a framing, which is then finished to match the bathroom, and with a removal panel to provide access to the pump, pipework and tanks.

PART THREE

3.1 COSTINGS

BCIS STAR RATING SYSTEM

The following tables are to be found with the costs for work in Part 3.

The star rating has been assessed on a scale of one to five stars; one star being the dearest, most disruptive, least energy savings, longest time to payback the initial outlay, five stars being the cheapest, least disruptive, most energy savings, shortest time to payback the initial outlay.

Generally, one star is a poor rating for the factor concerned while five stars is excellent.

In the costings box, one star reflects on the dearest items of work costing.

The Star rating system is defined below

BCIS STAR RATING

Rating £ = The cost of the work as shown in this part of the guide	
More than £10000	★
£5001 to £10000	★★
£1001 to £5000	★★★
£501 to £1000	★★★★
£1 to £500	★★★★★

Note that the ratings have been based on the value of works before any adjustments for grants, etc

Rating P = Payback period (Recovery of cost time)	
More than 100 years	★
51 years to 100 years	★★
26 to 50 years	★★★
11 to 25 years	★★★★
Up to 10 years	★★★★★

Rating E = Energy saving (Carbon saving*)

Up to £25 per annum	★
£26 to £50 per annum	★★
£51 to £75 per annum	★★★
£76 to £100 per annum	★★★★
More than £100 per annum	★★★★★

Note that the ratings have been based on the amount of time it will take to payback the initial outlay, by the savings in costs on fuel bills. As fuel bills rise this payback period period will reduce.
*The UK Government publishes conversion factors to determine the carbon dioxide emissions caused by the use of energy.

Rating D = Disruption costs to the householder whilst the works are being carried out

Major disruption to whole house	★
Major disruption to rooms or part of house	★★
Minor disruption to room/part of house	★★★
Little disruption, minor moving and making good	★★★★
No disruption	★★★★★

Note that the ratings are based on the degree of disruption to the house whilst the works are being carried out. This includes disruption both inside the property and externally.

Overall = The overall star rating for the item

Poor	★
Medium	★★
Good	★★★
Very Good	★★★★
Excellent	★★★★★

PASSIVE IMPROVEMENTS

PASSIVE IMPROVEMENTS		BCIS RATING				
		£	P	E	D	Overall
CAVITY AND EXTERNAL WALL INSULATION	Cavity wall insulation	★★★★	★★★★★	★★★★★	★★★★	★★★★★
	External wall insulation	★	★★	★★★★★	★★	★★★
IMPROVE WALL INSULATION	Insulation to internal skin of external wall	★★★	★★★	★★★★★	★	★★★
	Insulation to internal skin of external wall	★★★★	★★★	★★★★	★★	★★★
REPLACE AND IMPROVE ROOF INSULATION	Replace insulation to houses	★★★★★	★★★★★	★★★★★	★★★	★★★★★
	Improve insulation to houses	★★★★★	★★★★★	★★★★	★★★	★★★★
	Replace insulation to small areas	★★★★★	★★★★	★★	★★★	★★★★
	Improve insulation to small areas	★★★★★	★★★★	★	★★★	★★★★

PASSIVE IMPROVEMENTS		BCIS RATING				
		£	P	E	D	Overall
INSULATION TO GROUND FLOORS	Suspended timber floors: Install insulation, excluding removing floor covering to houses	★★	★★	★★	★	★★
	Suspended timber floors: Install insulation, excluding removing floor covering in small areas	★★★	★★	★★	★	★★
	Solid floors: Install insulation during construction of new extension	★★★★	★★	★★	★★★★★	★★★
WINDOWS	Replace individual windows with double glazed units	★★★	★★★★	★★★★	★★	★★★
	Seal window frames	★★★★★	★★★★	★	★★★★	★★★★
	Replace windows with double glazed units	★	★	★★★★	★★	★★
EXTERNAL DOORS AND FRAMES	Replace doors and frames	★★★	★★★★	★★★★	★★★	★★★★
	Install seals around door frames	★★★★★	★★★★	★	★★★★	★★★★

CONSERVA-TORIES,	Conserva-tories	★	★	★	★★★	★★
GARDEN ROOMS etc	Garden rooms	★	★	★	★★★	★★
PORCHES AND ROOFLIGHTS	Enclosed porches	★★	★★	★★	★★★	★★
	Rooflights	★★★	★★	★★	★★★	★★★

SUMMARY KEY TO BCIS STAR RATINGS

BCIS STAR RATING

£ = Cost

More than £10000	★
£5001 to £10000	★★
£1001 to £5000	★★★
£501 to £1000	★★★★
£1 to £500	★★★★★

P = Payback period (recovery of cost time)

More than 100 years	★
51 years to 100 years	★★
26 to 50 years	★★★
11 to 25 years	★★★★
Up to 10 years	★★★★★

E = Energy saving per year

Up to £25 p.a	★
£26 to £50 p.a	★★
£51 to £75 p.a.	★★★
£76 to £100 p.a.	★★★★
More than £100 p.a.	★★★★★

D = Disruption

Major disruption to whole house	★
Major disruption to rooms or part of house	★★
Minor disruption to room/part of house	★★★
Little disruption, minor moving and making good	★★★★
No disruption	★★★★★

Overall = Overall BCIS rating

Poor	★
Medium	★★
Good	★★★
Very Good	★★★★
Excellent	★★★★★

CAVITY AND EXTERNAL WALL INSULATION

Costs include VAT at 17.5%	HOUSE TYPE		
	Terraced	Semi Detached	Detached
	£	£	£

Cavity wall insulation

Inject cavity wall with foam or mineral fibre
system

	Terraced	Semi Detached	Detached
Front/ rear Elevation	220	410	600
Side Elevation	–	675	580
All Elevations	440	1500	2400

BCIS STAR RATING			
£	P	E	D
★★★★	★★★★★	★★★★★	★★★★
OVERALL STAR RATING ★★★★★			

External wall insulation

Replace/install insulation panel to external wall

Hack off render, replacing or installing new
insulation panel with rigid insulation board,
metal lathing and rendering to match existing

	Terraced	Semi Detached	Detached
Front/ rear Elevation	4110	8700	12850
Side Elevation	–	14100	12360
All Elevations	8220	31580	50430

BCIS STAR RATING			
£	P	E	D
★	★★	★★★★★	★★
OVERALL STAR RATING ★★★			

Hack off render, replacing or installing new
insulation panel with rigid insulation board,
metal lathing and rendering to match existing,
decorate one coat exterior stone paint

	Terraced	Semi Detached	Detached
Front/ rear Elevation	4350	9230	13620
Side Elevation	–	15040	13100
All Elevations	8700	33510	53440

Rates include scaffolding and protection

BCIS STAR RATING			
£	P	E	D
★	★★	★★★★★	★★
OVERALL STAR RATING ★★★			

IMPROVE WALL INSULATION

Costs include VAT at 17.5%

	HOUSE TYPE		
	Terraced	Semi Detached	Detached
	£	£	£

Insulation to internal skin of external wall

Take down plasterboard to internal skin,
install insulation, fix new plasterboard,
skim coat, skirting and decoration

	Terraced	Semi Detached	Detached
Front/ rear Elevation	**810**	**1755**	**2565**
Side Elevation	–	**4050**	**2025**
All Elevations	**1620**	**6390**	**9180**

BCIS STAR RATING			
£	P	E	D
★★★	★★★	★★★★★	★
OVERALL STAR RATING	★★★		

	Walls 2.75m high		
3m long	4m long	5m long	8m long
£	£	£	£

Insulation to internal skin of external wall

Take down plasterboard to internal skin,
install insulation, fix new plasterboard,
skim coat, skirting and decoration

3m long	4m long	5m long	8m long
450	**620**	**790**	**1240**

BCIS STAR RATING			
£	P	E	D
★★★★	★★★	★★★★	★★
OVERALL STAR RATING	★★★		

REPLACE AND IMPROVE ROOF INSULATION

Costs include VAT at 17.5%

	HOUSE TYPE		
	Terraced	Semi Detached	Detached
	£	£	£

Replace insulation

Clear out insulation and vacuum roof space
and lay 250mm thick glass fibre insulation
to roof space

| | 495 | 985 | 3440 |

BCIS STAR RATING			
£	P	E	D
★★★★★	★★★★★	★★★★★	★★★
OVERALL STAR RATING			★★★★★

Improve insulation level

Lay 150mm thick glass fibre insulation over
existing insulation

| | 325 | 555 | 1650 |

BCIS STAR RATING			
£	P	E	D
★★★★★	★★★★★	★★★★	★★★
OVERALL STAR RATING			★★★★

		Areas		
	m²	m²	m²	m²
	1	2	3	5
	£	£	£	£

Replace insulation

Clear out insulation and vacuum roof space
and lay 250mm thick glass fibre insulation
to roof space

| | 83 | 110 | 140 | 195 |

BCIS STAR RATING			
£	P	E	D
★★★★★	★★★★	★★	★★★
OVERALL STAR RATING			★★★★

Improve insulation level

Lay 150mm thick glass fibre insulation over
existing insulation

| | 70 | 86 | 100 | 130 |

BCIS STAR RATING			
£	P	E	D
★★★★★	★★★★	★	★★★
OVERALL STAR RATING			★★★★

PROVIDE WALKWAY IN ROOF SPACE

Costs include VAT at 17.5%

Length of Walkway (m)	Plywood £	RANGE	Softwood £

Install walkway in roof space for access to tanks etc.

Lay 1m wide timber flooring as walkway

Length of Walkway (m)	Plywood £		Softwood £
1	89	to	180
2	120	to	260
3	150	to	340
5	210	to	450

INSULATION TO GROUND FLOORS

Costs include VAT at 17.5%

	Terraced	Semi Detached	Detached
HOUSE TYPE	£	£	£

Suspended timber floors

Install insulation, excluding removing floor covering

	Terraced	Semi Detached	Detached
Lift floor boards, install insulation board with clips to joists, refix boards	860	1710	5100

Install insulation, including replacing floor covering

	Terraced	Semi Detached	Detached
Remove floor covering, lift floor boards, install insulation board with clips to joists, refix boards, relay new finishes			
Carpet PC£10 with underlay and PVC flooring	2040	4100	12200
Carpet PC£10 with underlay and QT flooring	2410	4650	13810
Carpet PC £10 with underlay and vitreous ceramic flooring	2440	4690	13940
Carpet PC£20 with underlay and PVC flooring	2180	4420	13170
Carpet PC£20 with underlay and QT flooring	2550	4970	14770
Carpet PC £20 with underlay and vitreous ceramic flooring	2580	5010	14900
Wood flooring and PVC flooring	2580	5340	15920
Wood flooring and QT flooring	2950	5890	17530
Wood flooring and ceramic flooring	2980	5930	17660

NOTE

	Terraced	Semi Detached	Detached
Ground floor finish, carpet or wood flooring except in following rooms	kitchen	kitchen cloaks	Kitchen utility cloaks

BCIS STAR RATING			
£	P	E	D
★★	★★	★★	★
OVERALL STAR RATING		★★	

INSULATION TO GROUND FLOORS

Costs include VAT at 17.5%

Suspended timber floors

Install insulation, excluding removing floor covering

	3 x 3m £	4 x 4m £	6 x 4m £
Lift floor boards, install insulation board with clips to joists, refix boards	390	695	1040

Install insulation, including replacing floor covering

Remove floor covering, lift floor boards, install insulation board with clips to joists, refix boards, relay new finishes

	3 x 3m	4 x 4m	6 x 4m
Carpet and underlay PC £10/m2	915	1630	2450
PC £20/m2	1010	1800	2700
PVC flooring, sheeting or tiles	860	1530	2300
Quarry tiles	1280	2270	3400
Vitreous ceramic tiles	1310	2330	3490
Wood flooring	1290	2290	3440

FLOORS TO ROOM — Room Size

BCIS STAR RATING			
£	P	E	D
★★★	★★	★★	★
OVERALL STAR RATING		★★	

Solid floors

Install insulation during construction of new extension

	3 x 3m £	4 x 4m £	6 x 4m £
Lay insulation board on new slab	235	420	625

Extension Size

BCIS STAR RATING			
£	P	E	D
★★★★	★★	★★	★★★★★
OVERALL STAR RATING		★★★	

WINDOWS

Costs include VAT at 17.5%

	600 x 900 £	900 x 900 £	900 x 1200 £	1200 x 1200 £	1500 x 1200 £	1800 x 1800 £
			Approximate window sizes			
Replace windows						
Take out and install double glazed window						
uPVC casement window	**270**	**385**	**465**	**630**	**880**	**1490**
uPVC sash window	**975**	**1260**	**1340**	**1870**	**2430**	**4270**
Take out and install window including double glazing and decorating externally						
Timber casement window	**480**	**590**	**660**	**710**	**1070**	**1670**
Metal casement window	**560**	**635**	**715**	**765**	**1140**	**1790**
Timber double hung sash window	**750**	**865**	**970**	**1230**	**1720**	-

BCIS STAR RATING			
£	P	E	D
★★★	★★★★	★★★★	★★
OVERALL STAR RATING		★★★	

WINDOWS

Costs include VAT at 17.5%

Single
Items
£

Seal to window frames

Install seal to sash window

Window size
600 x 900   **125**
1200 x 1200   **170**
1500 x 1200   **185**

BCIS STAR RATING			
£	P	E	D
★★★★★	★★★★	★	★★★★
OVERALL STAR RATING		★★★★	

WINDOWS AND DOORS

Costs include VAT at 17.5%

| | RANGE House Type | | |
	Terraced	Semi-Detached	Detached
	£	£	£
Replace windows			
Take out and install double glazed windows			
uPVC casement window	3820	7070	21140
uPVC sash window	11660	19400	62210
Take out and install windows including double glazing and decorating externally			
Timber casement window	4680	8020	24060
Metal casement window	5090	8570	25910
Timber double hung sash window	7890	13160	41330
Replace windows and doors			
Take out and install double glazed windows and doors			
uPVC casement window	5670	8920	23000
uPVC sash window	13510	21260	64070
Take out and install windows and doors including double glazing and decorating externally			
Timber casement window	6430	9770	26110
Metal casement window	6840	10320	27960
Timber double hung sash window	9630	14910	43380

BCIS STAR RATING			
£	P	E	D
★	★	★★★★	★★
OVERALL STAR RATING		★★	

EXTERNAL DOORS AND FRAMES

Costs include VAT at 17.5%

Single
Items
£

Replace doors and frames

Replace timber door and frame with uPVC door and frame

	Single Items £
Georgian panelled white door and frame	**840**
Georgian premier panelled white door with one glazed opening and frame	**1130**
Timber effect door with two glazed openings, frame and glazed light over	**1300**

BCIS STAR RATING			
£	P	E	D
★★★	★★★★	★★★★	★★★
OVERALL STAR RATING			★★★★

Seal to door frames

Install seal to single door frame

	Single Items £
Door frame jamb and head seal	**120**
External threshold seal with weather board strip	**75**
External threshold seal with weather board strip for door with water bar	**97**

BCIS STAR RATING			
£	P	E	D
★★★★★	★★★★	★	★★★★
OVERALL STAR RATING			★★★★

CONSERVATORIES, GARDEN ROOMS etc

Costs include VAT at 17.5%

	Floor Size m	RANGE £	to	£
CONSERVATORIES				
Excluding radiator	3 x 3	**10000**	to	**12500**
	4 x 4	**16000**	to	**21000**
	4 x 6	**23000**	to	**30500**
Including forming opening in existing external cavity wall and new pair of glazed doors, radiator	3 x 3	**12500**	to	**14500**
	4 x 4	**18500**	to	**23000**
	4 x 6	**25500**	to	**33000**

BCIS STAR RATING			
£	P	E	D
★	★	★	★★★
OVERALL STAR RATING			★★

	Floor Size m	RANGE £	to	£
GARDEN ROOMS				
Similar to conservatories but with solid roof including radiator	3 x 3	**10500**	to	**13000**
	4 x 4	**17000**	to	**22000**
	4 x 6	**24500**	to	**32000**
Including forming opening in existing external cavity wall and new pair of glazed doors, radiator	3 x 3	**13000**	to	**15500**
	4 x 4	**19500**	to	**24500**
	4 x 6	**27000**	to	**34000**

BCIS STAR RATING			
£	P	E	D
★	★	★	★★★
OVERALL STAR RATING			★★

PORCHES AND ROOFLIGHTS

Costs include VAT at 17.5%

	Size m2	£	RANGE Quality of Materials		£

Enclosed porches
Purpose built uPVC on concrete base

	Size	£		£
	2 x 1	**3400**	to	**8600**
	3 x 2.5	**5900**	to	**12000**

Brick and timber with uPVC doors and windows

	2 x 1	**5500**	to	**7500**
	3 x 2.5	**10500**	to	**13000**

BCIS STAR RATING			
£	P	E	D
**	**	**	***
OVERALL STAR RATING		**	

Rooflights

Velux rooflight with framing and plasterboard — 0.9 x 1.2 — **1800** to **2500**

BCIS STAR RATING			
£	P	E	D
***	**	**	***
OVERALL STAR RATING		***	

REPLACEMENT OF EXISTING EQUIPMENT

REPLACEMENT OF EXISTING EQUIPMENT		BCIS RATING				
		£	P	E	D	Overall
REPLACE HEATING SYSTEM	Replace heating system excluding pipework	★★	★★★	★★★★	★★	★★★
	Replace heating system including pipework	★★	★★★	★★★★★	★	★★★
REPLACE FAULTY EQUIPMENT	Replace boiler	★★★	★★★	★★★	★★★	★★★
	Replace radiators including reconnection and rebalancing	★★★★★	★★★	★★★	★★★	★★★
	Replace radiator valves	★★★★★	★★★★	★★★	★★★★	★★★★
	Replace central heating controls	★★★★★	★★★	★★★	★★★★	★★★★
INSULATION BEHIND RADIATORS	Install radiator heat reflector foil to wall behind radiator	★★★★★	★★★★	★	★★★★	★★★★
	Install radiator heat reflector foil to wall behind all radiators	★★★★★	★★★★	★★	★★★★	★★★★
REPLACE BOILERS	Stoves	★★★	★★★	★★	★★★	★★★
	Boilers, installed and fitted to existing system	★★	★★★	★★★★	★★★	★★★
	Wood chip boiler	★	★★★	★★★★	★★★	★★★

REPLACEMENT OF EXISTING EQUIPMENT		BCIS RATING				
		£	P	E	D	Overall
EXTERNAL WATER MAIN INSIDE PROPERTY BOUNDARY	Replace leaking pipe	★★★	★★	★★★★	★★★	★★★
	Replace short length of leaking pipe	★★★★	★★	★★★★	★★★	★★★
EXTERNAL WATER MAIN INSIDE PROPERTY	Replace leaking pipe	★★	★★	★★★★	★	★★
	Replace short length of leaking pipe	★★★★★	★★★★	★★★★	★★	★★★★
WATER FITTINGS INSIDE PROPERTY	Replace faulty fittings	★★★★★	★★★★	★★	★★★	★★★★
	Replace existing with new energy saving fittings	★★★★★	★★★★	★★	★★★	★★★★
REPLACE MISSING OR DAMAGED INSULATION	Replace insulating jacket around the cold water tank	★★★★★	★★★	★	★★★★★	★★★★
	Replace insulation to pipework in roofspace	★★★★★	★★★★	★	★★★★	★★★★
	Replace insulation to pipework under floors	★★★★★	★★★★	★	★★	★★★
ELECTRICAL FITTINGS INSIDE PROPERTY	Lighting	★★★★★	★★★★★	★★	★★★★★	★★★★
	Time control switched, immersion heaters	★★★★★	★★★★★	★★	★★★★★	★★★★
	Replace light bulbs	★★★★★	★★★★★	★	★★★★★	★★★★

SUMMARY KEY TO BCIS STAR RATINGS

BCIS STAR RATING

£ = Cost

More than £10000	★
£5001 to £10000	★★
£1001 to £5000	★★★
£501 to £1000	★★★★
£1 to £500	★★★★★

P = Payback period (recovery of cost time)

More than 100 years	★
51 years to 100 years	★★
26 to 50 years	★★★
11 to 25 years	★★★★
Up to 10 years	★★★★★

E = Energy saving per year

Up to £25 p.a	★
£26 to £50 p.a	★★
£51 to £75 p.a.	★★★
£76 to £100 p.a.	★★★★
More than £100 p.a.	★★★★★

D = Disruption

Major disruption to whole house	★
Major disruption to rooms or part of house	★★
Minor disruption to room/part of house	★★★
Little disruption, minor moving and making good	★★★★
No disruption	★★★★★

Overall = Overall BCIS rating

Poor	★
Medium	★★
Good	★★★
Very Good	★★★★
Excellent	★★★★★

REPLACE HEATING SYSTEM

Costs include VAT at 17.5%

Replace heating system excluding pipework

Wall mounted boiler, single and double panel
radiators, wall thermostat and programmer

	HOUSE TYPE		
	Terraced	Semi Detached	Detached
	£	£	£
Clockwork programmer	4420	5550	6980
Digital programmer	5150	6280	7710

BCIS STAR RATING			
£	P	E	D
★★	★★★	★★★★	★★
OVERALL STAR RATING		★★★	

Replace heating system including pipework

Wall mounted boiler, single and double panel
radiators, pipework, wall thermostat and
programmer

	Terraced	Semi Detached	Detached
Clockwork programmer	6410	7990	10510
Digital programmer	7140	8700	11240

BCIS STAR RATING			
£	P	E	D
★★	★★	★★★★★	★
OVERALL STAR RATING		★★★	

REPLACE FAULTY EQUIPMENT

Costs include VAT at 17.5%

Single
Items
£

Replace boiler

Replace wall mounted boiler, including draining down
system and connecting to flue and pipework

1720

Replace free standing boiler, including draining down
system and connecting to flue and pipework

4770

BCIS STAR RATING			
£	P	E	D
★★★	★★★	★★★	★★★
OVERALL STAR RATING			★★★

Replace radiators including reconnection and rebalancing

Single panel 400 x 600mm	**185**
Single panel 500 x 1000mm	**235**
Single panel 600 x 1800mm	**360**
Double panel 400 x 500mm	**250**
Double panel 500 x 1200mm	**405**
Double panel 600 x 1600mm	**530**

BCIS STAR RATING			
£	P	E	D
★★★★★	★★★★	★★★	★★★★
OVERALL STAR RATING			★★★★

Replace radiator valves

Replace radiator valves	**110**
Replace thermostatic radiator valve	**120**

BCIS STAR RATING			
£	P	E	D
★★★★★	★★★★	★★★	★★★★
OVERALL STAR RATING			★★★★

REPLACE FAULTY EQUIPMENT (Contd)

Single
Items
£

Replace central heating controls

Cylinder thermostat	**94**
Wall thermostat	**100**
Programmer (clockwork)	**225**
Programmer (digital)	**955**

BCIS STAR RATING			
£	P	E	D
★★★★★	★★★	★★★	★★★★
OVERALL STAR RATING		★★★★	

Cleaning central heating system

Powerflush system	**350**

Storage heaters

Overhaul, including inspecting fusible link, replace thermostat, resetting thermal cutout and checking cable and testing	**150**

INSULATION BEHIND RADIATORS

Costs include VAT at 17.5%

Install radiator heat reflector foil to wall behind radiator

Radiator size

	Single Items £
single panel 400 x 600mm	**53**
single panel 500 x 1000mm	**54**
single panel 600 x 1800mm	**57**

BCIS STAR RATING			
£	P	E	D
★★★★★	★★★★	★	★★★★
OVERALL STAR RATING			★★★★

	HOUSE TYPE		
	Terraced £	Semi Detached £	Detached £
Install radiator reflector foil behind all radiators	**195**	**270**	**350**

BCIS STAR RATING			
£	P	E	D
★★★★★	★★★★	★★	★★★★
OVERALL STAR RATING			★★★★

REPLACE BOILERS

Biomass

Stoves
Install 3Kw room stove including stainless steel liner to flue

	RANGE Design of Stove	
£		£
1600	**to**	**2000**

BCIS STAR RATING			
£	P	E	D
★★★	★★★	★★	★★★
OVERALL STAR RATING		★★★	

Boilers, installed and fitted to existing system, appropriate for a terraced, semi detached and detached house

	RANGE Dependent upon quality, type and location	
£		£

Boilers, installed and fitted to existing system
Logs
14 - 25Kw interlinked to existing oil or gas boiler

4500	**to**	**12000**

Wood pellets boiler
14 - 25Kw with auto feed and start, location adjacent to existing pipework, removal of existing boiler

6200	**to**	**14500**

Combined wood pellets/logs boiler
14 - 25Kw for existing open hot water system pipework, removal of existing boiler

		6600

BCIS STAR RATING			
£	P	E	D
★★	★★★	★★★★	★★★
OVERALL STAR RATING		★★★	

REPLACE BOILERS (Contd)

	Single Items £
Wood chips boiler	
20Kw with auto feed and start, location adjacent to existing pipework, removal of existing boiler	**23000**
Storage for wood pellets	
200 litre	**400**
500 litre	**640**

BCIS STAR RATING			
£	P	E	D
★	★★★	★★★★	★★★
OVERALL STAR RATING		★★★	

EXTERNAL WATER MAIN INSIDE PROPERTY BOUNDARY

Costs include VAT at 17.5%

	5 £	10 £	15 £	20 £
Length of Pipework (m)				

Replace leaking pipe

Replace pipe, excavating and making good in the following surfaces

	5 £	10 £	15 £	20 £
Soft surface	415	685	955	1215
Concrete or paving slabs surface	540	1075	1610	2145
Tarmac surface	530	1060	1580	2100
Clay paviors surface	585	1170	1760	2340

BCIS STAR RATING			
£	P	E	D
★★★	★★	★★★★	★★★
OVERALL STAR RATING		★★★	

Length of Pipework (m)

	1 £	2 £	3 £	5 £
Replace short length of pipe, excavating and making good in the following surfaces				
Soft surface	115	185	255	395
Concrete or paving slabs surface	160	265	370	580
Tarmac surface	165	280	395	625
Clay paviors surface	180	305	430	680

BCIS STAR RATING			
£	P	E	D
★★★★	★★	★★★★	★★★
OVERALL STAR RATING		★★★	

WATER SUPPLY PIPEWORK INSIDE PROPERTY

Costs include VAT at 17.5%

Replace hot and cold water systems

	RANGE		
	£		£
Replace all hot and cold water pipework, storage cistern, expansion tank, hot water cylinder, immersion heater, connecting pipework to existing sanitary fittings	**2370**	**to**	**3570**
As above, but including new sanitary fittings	**4700**	**to**	**9950**

BCIS STAR RATING			
£	P	E	D
★★	★★	★★★★	★
OVERALL STAR RATING		★★	

Replace pipework

	Length of Pipework (m)			
	1	2	5	10
	£	£	£	£
Cut out and replace exposed copper pipework	**105**	**155**	–	–
Cut out and replace concealed copper pipework, behind access panel or the like	**125**	**200**	–	–

BCIS STAR RATING			
£	P	E	D
★★★★★	★★★★	★★★★	★★
OVERALL STAR RATING		★★★★	

FITTINGS INSIDE PROPERTY

	Single Items £
Costs include VAT at 17.5%	
Replace faulty fittings	
Replace cold water storage cistern or tank and lid, 27l capacity	**250**
Replace cold water storage cistern or tank and lid, 45l capacity	**440**
Remove existing and install hot water cylinder size 1200 x 450mm and connect all pipework	**385**
Remove existing and install immersion heater	**140**
Replace ball cock to cold water tank	**120**
Replace shower head and bracket	**90**
Replace flexible shower hose	**74**
Renew ball valve including plastic float	**130**
Renew plastic syphonage unit to high or low level cisterns	**110**
Fit replacement washer to ball valve	**67**
Fit replacement washer to tap	**67**

BCIS STAR RATING			
£	P	E	D
★★★★★	★★★★	★★	★★★
OVERALL STAR RATING		★★★★	

FITTINGS INSIDE PROPERTY (Contd)

Replace existing with new energy saving fittings

	Single Items £
Replace low level cistern with new water saving cistern	**200**
Replace high level cistern with new water saving cistern	**205**
WC suite with low level water saving cistern and seat	**610**
Replace basin pillar tap with new to match existing	**195**
Replace bib tap with new to match existing	**205**
Replace basin mixer	**255**
Replace bath mixer	**300**
Supply and fit flush control valve with infra red detector and copper pipework	**415**

BCIS STAR RATING			
£	P	E	D
★★★★★	★★★★	★★	★★★
OVERALL STAR RATING		★★★★	

REPLACE MISSING OR DAMAGED INSULATION

Costs include VAT at 17.5%	RANGE Per Jacket		
	£		£

Replace insulating jacket around cold water tank

Remove existing and install 60mm thick polyethylene insulating jacket complete with fixing bands	**245**	**to**	**305**

Replace insulating jacket around hot water cylinder

Replace jacket to hot water cylinder including fixing 80mm thick flame retardent PVC complete with fixing bands	**110**	**to**	**135**

BCIS STAR RATING			
£	P	E	D
★★★★★	★★★	★	★★★★★
OVERALL STAR RATING		★★★★	

	Length of Pipework (m)			
	1	2	5	10
	£	£	£	£
Replace insulation to pipework				
Pipework in roof space or cupboards	**73**	**85**	**110**	**170**

BCIS STAR RATING			
£	P	E	D
★★★★★	★★★★	★	★★★★
OVERALL STAR RATING		★★★★	

Pipework under floors

	1	2	5	10
Pipes running in direction of floor boarding	**79**	**98**	**145**	**240**
Pipes running across direction of floor boarding	**120**	**175**	**325**	**550**

BCIS STAR RATING			
£	P	E	D
★★★★★	★★★★	★	★★
OVERALL STAR RATING		★★★	

REPLACE FAULTY ELECTRICAL FITTINGS

Costs include VAT at 17.5%

Single
Items
£

Lighting

Overhaul faulty lighting main switch including
isolating and reconnecting supply, cleaning
contacts and testing

79

Trace fault on wiring circuit

75

BCIS STAR RATING			
£	P	E	D
★★★★★	★★★★★	★★	★★★★★
OVERALL STAR RATING		★★★★	

Replace faulty equipment

Renew time control switch and test

145

Renew immersion heater, isolate supply, drain
tank, disconnect and connect heater and test:

Top heater

99

Bottom heater

120

Instant water heaters
Inspect and repair faulty heater

73

BCIS STAR RATING			
£	P	E	D
★★★★★	★★★★★	★★	★★★★★
OVERALL STAR RATING		★★★★	

REPLACE ELECTRICAL EQUIPMENT

Costs include VAT at 17.5%

			RANGE	
		£		£

Replace bulbs

Low energy bulbs, **supply guide prices**

To replace standard bulbs	with low energy bulbs			
40W	8W	4	to	8
60W	11W	4	to	8
75W	18W	4	to	8
100w	20W	4	to	8

To replace candle bulbs				
25W	5W	4	to	5
35W	7W	5	to	8
45W	9W	5	to	12

To replace spotlight bulbs				
40W	7W	10	to	15
60W	11W	10	to	15
75W	15W	10	to	18
120W	20W	10	to	18

To replace halogen lamps				
35W	7W	5	to	11
50W	11W	9	to	16
75W	50W	3	to	9

These prices are decreasing as major supermarkets and DIY stores are stocking these items in larger quantities.

BCIS STAR RATING			
£	P	E	D
★★★★★	★★★★★ ★		★★★★★
OVERALL STAR RATING	★★★★		

ACTIVE IMPROVEMENTS

ACTIVE IMPROVEMENTS		BCIS RATING				
		£	P	E	D	Overall
HEATING	Solar panels	★★★	★	★	★★	★★
	Heat pumps	★★	★★★	★★	★★	★★★
POWER	Photovoltaic panels	★	★★	★★★	★★	★★
	Wind turbines	★	★★	★★★★★	★★	★★
	Small turbine to supplement mains electricity supply	★★★	★★★★	★★★★	★★	★★★
RAINWATER HARVESTING	Butt and tanks above ground	★★★★★	★★★★★	★	★★★★	★★★★
	Tanks below ground	★★★	★★★	★★	★★	★★★

SUMMARY KEY TO BCIS STAR RATINGS

BCIS STAR RATING

£ = Cost

More than £10000	★
£5001 to £10000	★★
£1001 to £5000	★★★
£501 to £1000	★★★★
£1 to £500	★★★★★

P = Payback period (recovery of cost time)

More than 100 years	★
51 years to 100 years	★★
26 to 50 years	★★★
11 to 25 years	★★★★
Up to 10 years	★★★★★

E = Energy saving per year

Up to £25 p.a	★
£26 to £50 p.a	★★
£51 to £75 p.a.	★★★
£76 to £100 p.a.	★★★★
More than £100 p.a.	★★★★★

D = Disruption

Major disruption to whole house	★
Major disruption to rooms or part of house	★★
Minor disruption to room/part of house	★★★
Little disruption, minor moving and making good	★★★★
No disruption	★★★★★

Overall = Overall BCIS rating

Poor	★
Medium	★★
Good	★★★
Very Good	★★★★
Excellent	★★★★★

HEATING

	HOUSE TYPE		
	Terraced	Semi Detached	Detached
	£	£	£

Solar panels

Installation of panels to roof and connection to hot water system including all necessary scaffolding and making good

Terraced	Semi Detached	Detached
4000	4000	5000

BCIS STAR RATING			
£	P	E	D
★★★	★	★	★★
OVERALL STAR RATING			★★

Heat pumps

Costs are based on the assumption that the property has a central heating system that is either new or no more than one or two year's old. The hot water system assumes a tank size of 180 litres

Ground source

Horizontal system

Terraced	Semi Detached	Detached
8000 to 10000	9000 to 11000	9500 to 11500

Vertical system

Terraced	Semi Detached	Detached
11500 to 13500	14500 to 16500	17000 to 19000

Air source

Terraced	Semi Detached	Detached
7500 to 9500	7750 to 9750	8000 to 10000

BCIS STAR RATING			
£	P	E	D
★★	★★★	★★★★★	★★
OVERALL STAR RATING			★★★

POWER

	HOUSE TYPE		
	Terraced	Semi Detached	Detached
Photovoltaic panels	£	£	£

Installation and connection including all scaffolding and making good

1.5Kw	**8000 to 9000**	—	—
2Kw		**10000 to 12000**	
5Kw			**25000**

BCIS STAR RATING			
£	P	E	D
★	★★	★★★	★★
OVERALL STAR RATING			★★

Wind turbines

Installation and connection of freestanding turbine including making good

3Kw	**11000 to 12000**	—	—
5Kw		**16000**	
6Kw			**20000**

BCIS STAR RATING			
£	P	E	D
★	★★	★★★★★	★★
OVERALL STAR RATING			★★

	Single Items
	£
Small turbine to supplement mains electricity supply	
1.2Kw	**2000**

BCIS STAR RATING			
£	P	E	D
★★★	★★★★	★★★★	★★
OVERALL STAR RATING			★★★

RAINWATER HARVESTING

Costs include VAT at 17.5%	Single Items £

Butts and tanks above ground

Install rainwater butt on base, including cutting downpipe, fitting diverter and overflow	**65**

Install 700 litre rainwater tank, including cutting downpipe, fitting diverter and overflow	**310**

BCIS STAR RATING			
£	P	E	D
★★★★★	★★★★★★	★★★★
OVERALL STAR RATING		★★★★	

	HOUSE TYPE		
Terraced £	Semi Detached £	Detached £

Butts and tanks above ground

Installation of tank and pump, connection to existing WCs, washing machine etc, and making good	**3200**	**3200**	**4500**

BCIS STAR RATING			
£	P	E	D
★★★	★★★	★★	★★
OVERALL STAR RATING		★★★	

ALL RATINGS SUMMARY TABLE

BCIS STAR RATING SUMMARY TABLE

NATURE OF ACTIVITY	ITEM	DESCRIPTION
REPLACEMENT	REPLACE MISSING OR DAMAGED INSULATION	Replace insulation to pipework in roof space
		Replace insulating jacket around cold water tank
		Replace insulation to pipework under floors
	REPLACE FAULTY EQUIPMENT	Replace radiator valves
	ELECTRICAL FITTINGS INSIDE PROPERTY	Lighting
		Time control switched, immersion heaters
		Replace lightbulbs
PASSIVE	REPLACE AND IMPROVE ROOF INSULATION	Replace insulation to houses
		Replace insulation to small areas
		Improve insulation to houses
		Improve insulation to small areas
	WINDOWS	Seal window frames
	EXTERNAL DOORS AND FRAMES	Install seals around door frames
	CAVITY AND EXTERNAL WALL INSULATION	Cavity wall insulation
	INSULATION TO THE GROUND FLOORS	Solid floors: Install insulation during construction of new extension
	EXTERNAL DOORS AND FRAMES	Replace doors and frames
	IMPROVE WALL INSULATION	Insulation to internal partition of external wall
	CAVITY AND EXTERNAL WALL INSULATION	External wall insulation
	INSULATION TO GROUND FLOORS	Suspended timber floors: Install insulation, excluding removing floor covering in small areas
		Suspended timber floors: Install insulation, excluding removing floor covering to houses

BCIS STAR RATING SUMMARY TABLE

£	P	E	D	OVERALL
★★★★★	★★★★	★	★★★★	★★★★
★★★★★	★★★	★	★★★★★	★★★★
★★★★★	★★★★	★	★★	★★★
★★★★★	★★★★	★★★	★★★★	★★★★
★★★★★	★★★★★	★★	★★★★★	★★★★
★★★★★	★★★★★	★★	★★★★★	★★★★
★★★★★	★★★★★	★	★★★★★	★★★★
★★★★★	★★★★★	★★★★★	★★★	★★★★★★
★★★★★	★★★★	★★	★★★	★★★★
★★★★★	★★★★★	★★★★	★★★	★★★★
★★★★★	★★★★	★	★★★	★★★★
★★★★★	★★★★	★	★★★★	★★★★
★★★★★	★★★★	★	★★★★	★★★★
★★★★	★★★★★	★★★★★	★★★★	★★★★★
★★★★	★★	★★	★★★★★	★★★
★★★	★★★★	★★★★	★★★	★★★★
★★★★	★★★	★★★★	★★	★★★
★	★★	★★★★★	★★	★★★
★★★	★★	★★	★	★★
★★	★★	★★	★	★★

BCIS STAR RATING SUMMARY TABLE

NATURE OF ACTIVITY	ITEM	DESCRIPTION
PASSIVE	IMPROVE WALL INSULATION	Insulation to internal skin of external wall
	WINDOWS	Replace individual windows with double glazed units
		Replace windows with double glazed units
REPLACEMENT	INSULATION BEHIND RADIATORS	Install radiator heat reflector foil to wall behind radiator
		Install radiator heat reflector foil to wall behind all radiators
	REPLACE BOILERS	Boilers, installed and fitted to existing system
		Wood chip boiler
	REPLACE FAULTY EQUIPMENT	Replace radiators including reconnection and rebalancing
	EXTERNAL WATER MAIN INSIDE PROPERTY	Replace short length of leaking pipe
	WATER FITTINGS INSIDE PROPERTY	Replace existing with new energy saving fittings
	REPLACE HEATING SYSTEM	Replace heating system excluding pipework
	REPLACE FAULTY EQUIPMENT	Replace boiler
		Replace central heating controls
	EXTERNAL WATER MAIN INSIDE PROPERTY BOUNDARY	Replace short length of leaking pipe
	WATER FITTINGS INSIDE PROPERTY	Replace faulty fittings
	REPLACE BOILERS	Stoves

BCIS STAR RATING SUMMARY TABLE

£	P	E	D	OVERALL
★★★	★★	★★★★★	★	★★★
★★★	★★★★	★★★★	★★	★★★
★	★	★★★★	★★	★★
★★★★★	★★★★	★★	★★★★	★★★★
★★★★★	★★★	★	★★★★	★★★★
★★	★★★	★★★★	★★★	★★★
★	★★★	★★★★	★★★	★★★
★★★★★	★★★	★★★	★★★	★★★
★★★★★	★★★★	★★★★	★★	★★★★
★★★★★	★★★★	★★	★★★	★★★★
★★	★★★	★★★★	★★	★★★
★★★	★★★	★★★	★★★	★★★
★★★★★	★★★	★★★	★★★★	★★★★
★★★★	★★	★★★★	★★★	★★★
★★★★★	★★★★	★★	★★★	★★★★
★★★	★★★	★★	★★★	★★★

BCIS STAR RATING SUMMARY TABLE

NATURE OF ACTIVITY	ITEM	DESCRIPTION
ACTIVE	RAINWATER HARVESTING	Butts and tanks above ground
PASSIVE	PORCHES AND ROOFLIGHTS	Enclosed porches Rooflights
REPLACEMENT	REPLACE HEATING SYSTEM EXTERNAL WATER MAIN INSIDE PROPERTY BOUNDARY	Replace heating system including pipework Replace leaking pipe
ACTIVE	HEATING	Solar panels Heat pumps
	POWER	Photovoltaic panels Wind turbines Small turbine to supplement mains electricity supply
	RAINWATER HARVESTING	Tanks below ground
REPLACEMENT	EXTERNAL WATER MAIN INSIDE PROPERTY	Replace leaking pipe
PASSIVE	CONSERVA-TORIES, GARDEN ROOMS ETC.	Conservatories Garden rooms

BCIS STAR RATING SUMMARY TABLE

£	P	E	D	OVERALL
★★★★★	★★★★★	★	★★★★	★★★★
★★	★★	★★	★★★	★★
★★★	★★	★★	★★★	★★★
★★	★★★	★★★★★	★	★★★
★★★	★★	★★★★	★★★	★★★
★★★	★	★	★★	★★
★★	★★★	★★	★★	★★★
★	★★	★★★	★★	★★
★	★★	★★★★★	★★	★★
★★★	★★★★	★★★★	★★	★★★
★★★	★★★	★★	★★	★★★
★★	★★	★★★★	★	★
★	★	★	★★★	★★
★	★	★	★★★	★★★

SUMMARY KEY TO BCIS STAR RATINGS

BCIS STAR RATING

£ = Cost

More than £10000	★
£5001 to £10000	★★
£1001 to £5000	★★★
£501 to £1000	★★★★
£1 to £500	★★★★★

P = Payback period (recovery of cost time)

More than 100 years	★
51 years to 100 years	★★
26 to 50 years	★★★
11 to 25 years	★★★★
Up to 10 years	★★★★★

E = Energy saving per year

Up to £25 p.a	★
£26 to £50 p.a	★★
£51 to £75 p.a.	★★★
£76 to £100 p.a.	★★★★
More than £100 p.a.	★★★★★

D = Disruption

Major disruption to whole house	★
Major disruption to rooms or part of house	★★
Minor disruption to room/part of house	★★★
Little disruption, minor moving and making good	★★★★
No disruption	★★★★★

Overall = Overall BCIS rating

Poor	★
Medium	★★
Good	★★★
Very Good	★★★★
Excellent	★★★★★

The Greener Homes Price Guide - Errata Slip

page 113
3.2 PAYBACK PERIODS

Item	Payback Period Years
Cavity wall insulation to external walls	3
Increase insulation in loft additional 150mm thick	5
Insulation to timber suspended ground floor	60
Replace existing inadequate hot water cylinder and pipework insulation	20
Install condensing boiler to replace existing boiler, including all adaptations to existing plumbing	18
Install full central heating controls package including digital programmer, thermostatic radiator valves and alterations	30
Replace single glazed windows with double glazed units including new double glazed doors and make good	>100
Installation of solar panels including all plumbing alterations and making good	>100

page 115
3.3 ENERGY SAVINGS

Item	Saving per annum £
Install condensing boiler to replace existing boiler, including all adaptations to existing plumbing	95

3.2 PAYBACK PERIODS

Introduction

The payback period is the time taken for the initial outlay cost to be recovered. Dependent on the time it takes to recover this cost, other factors may also need to be factored in with the initial outlay cost. These will include any necessary cleaning, servicing in accordance with the manufacturer's recommendations and the replacement of any parts that may become defective during the payback period.

Photovoltaic and solar panels will require cleaning on a periodic basis. This cleaning will depend upon the location of the property. If the property is in close proximity to a main road or trees then the cleaning of the panels will be required on a more regular basis than a property located in a quiet rural location with no trees.

Payback periods

The following is a list of estimated payback periods for energy saving products for a terraced house included in this guide.

The initial outlay costs include VAT at 17.5%; no adjustment being made for the present rate of 5%, at the time of writing. The grants, which may be currently available to householders, have also not been included in the outlay costs. Maintenance, servicing and parts replacement have been assessed and included in the outlay.

Fuel costs have been assessed from the increases over the past few years. It is not inconceivable, however, that these costs may increase far more rapidly over the next 10, 20 or 50 years, as natural fuel resources dwindle, and the payback periods will be reduced correspondingly by the effect of these increases.

Item	Payback Period Years
Cavity wall insulation to external walls	5
Increase insulation in loft, additional 150mm thick	13
Insulation to timber suspended ground floor	61
Replace existing inadequate hot water cylinder and pipework insulation	38
Install condensing boiler to replace existing boiler, including all adaptations to existing plumbing	38
Installation of full central heating controls package including digital programmer, thermostatic radiator valves and alterations	34
Replace single glazed windows with double glazed units including new double glazed doors and all making good	124
Installation of solar panels including all plumbing alterations and making good	208

The beginning of 2008 has seen a greater increase in fuel bills than in previous years and this is now expected to be the trend in the following months, and possibly years. The payback periods, as a consequence, will similarly fall from the figures shown, and many of the energy saving devices will now be far more advantageous and attractive to the homeowner.

The Energy Saving Trust (web site: http://www.energysavingtrust.org.uk/) has also listed Payback Periods on their web site. These have been produced for a three bedroom semi detached house, with adjustments made for current legislation regarding grants and VAT. No allowances have been made in their figures, however, for builder's work in connection with the installations, general maintenance, servicing and repair costs.

3.3 ENERGY SAVINGS

Introduction

The following is a list of estimated energy saving per annum per product for a terraced house included in this guide.

The initial outlay costs include VAT at 17.5%, no adjustment being made for the present rate of 5%, at the time of writing. The grants, which may be currently available to householders, have also not been included in the outlay costs. Maintenance, servicing and parts replacement have been assessed and included in the outlay.

Fuel costs have been assessed from the increases over the past few years. It is not inconceivable however that these costs may increase far more rapidly over the next 10, 20 or 50 years, as natural fuel resources dwindle, and the payback periods will correspondingly be reduced by the effect of these increases. The recent large increases in fuel bills at the beginning of 2008 confirm that the costs are now increasing more rapidly and this trend is expected to continue. The savings per annum will therefore increase with every increase in these bills.

Item	Saving per annum £
Cavity wall insulation to external walls	145
Increase insulation in loft, additional 150mm thick	60
Insulation to timber suspended ground floor	45
Replace existing inadequate hot water cylinder and pipework insulation.	20
Install condensing boiler to replace existing boiler, including all adaptations to existing plumbing	52
Installation of full central heating controls package including digital programmer, thermostatic radiator valves and alterations	65
Replace single glazed windows with double glazed units including new double glazed doors and all making good	75
Installation of solar panels including all plumbing alterations and making good	24
Installation of photovoltaic panels including all electrical alterations and making good	75
Replace existing boiler with Biomass including all alterations and making good	180

The Energy Saving Trust (web site: http://www.energysavingtrust.org. uk/) has also listed energy savings per annum on their web site. These have been produced for a three bedroom semi detached house, with adjustments made for current legislation regarding grants and VAT. No allowances have been made in their figures however for builder's work in connection with the installations, general maintenance, servicing and repair costs.

3.4 SAP HOME ENERGY RATING AND ENERGY PERFORMANCE CERTIFICATES

SAPS

SAP stands for Standard Assessment Procedure, which is an energy rating for housing. This is based on the Building Research Establishment Domestic Energy Model, commonly called BREDEM, which calculates the annual energy requirements of housing and takes into account space and water heating.

A SAP rating is required for all new build dwellings and those undergoing significant material alteration (such as the addition of an extension to the dwelling).

The SAP rating has a scale of 1 to 100; 1 being very poor, 100 being excellent. A typical SAP rating for an average house in England is around 45. A rating on a house built to current building regulations would be closer to 80 SAP points. Ratings for newly constructed homes are assessed from plan at the design stage and at the as built stage. Similarly, existing dwellings being extended can also be assessed from scale drawings, but conversions will require a site visit.

How SAP Ratings Compare to the A-G Scale

Rating	Scale
1 to 20	G
21 to 38	F
39 to 54	E
55 to 68	D
69 to 80	C
81 to 91	B

The costs of obtaining a report for an existing normal size dwelling with up to three bedrooms will start at around £500, excluding Value Added Tax. This cost will include the initial consultation, an energy performance assessment of the existing dwelling, and modelling of the performance for a notional dwelling to include extension or improvements and all print off's for building control compliance.

SAP ratings form part of the Energy Performance Certificates.

Energy Performance Certificates (EPCs)

The Energy Performance Certificate (EPC) tells you how efficient your dwelling is in its existing condition and how it forms part of the Home Information Pack (HIP).

The home inspector will survey a dwelling in order to produce the EPC. The EPC provides details of the average costs for heating, hot water and lighting in the home. It also rates the energy performance of the home and provides useful information on how to improve the efficiency of the dwelling, which could mean lower energy bills. It will also show the dwelling's impact on the environment, which is primarily assessed on the type of fuel used to heat both the home and the hot water.

Energy Performance Certificates tell you how energy efficient the dwelling is on a scale of A-G. The most efficient homes - which should have the lowest fuel bills - are in band A. The Certificate also tells you, again on a scale of A-G, about the impact the home has on the environment. The better-rated homes should have less impact through carbon dioxide (CO_2) emissions. The average property in the UK is in bands D-E for both ratings. The Certificate also includes recommendations on ways to improve the home's energy efficiency to save money and help the environment. There are several improvements that can be made to any home, particularly older dwellings, to reduce the environmental carbon footprint by reducing carbon emissions. Fuel bills could be reduced simply by adopting a few simple measures such as increasing the thickness of loft insulation to current requirements, having cavity wall insulation injected into cavity walls, installing a hot water cylinder jacket, replacing an old boiler with a new energy efficient boiler and replacing existing radiator valves with thermostatic radiator valves.

3.5 CARBON FOOTPRINT

The carbon footprint is a measure of the amount of carbon dioxide which is emitted from a dwelling by burning fossil fuels and of the impact carbon emitting human activities have on the environment. It's usually measured in tonnes of carbon dioxide emitted on a yearly basis.

There are several ways to reduce a dwelling's carbon footprint. The single most important factor is the type of fuel used to provide hot water and to heat the home.

The most common form of domestic heating in dwellings in the United Kingdom is 'central heating' which comprises a gas boiler using mains gas as its fuel. Other forms of fuel used are coal, smokeless fuel, oil, wood, and electricity.

Carbon coal based or fossil fuels can reduce the EPC rating significantly and increase the footprint, although coal fired heating systems will have a worse impact on the EPC rating than any other type of fuel because when burned it creates greater carbon emissions than, for example, gas fired heating systems. CO2 emissions can be reduced, the footprint improved, and the environmental impact reduced by not using coal based energy products.

Not all gas appliances are efficient; back boilers, for example, have a poor rating and are approximately 70% efficient, whereas a new gas condensing boiler is over 90% efficient. Therefore, even though both appliances are fuelled by gas, more carbon is produced by the back boiler.

A household's carbon footprint can be calculated by visiting the Government's website: http://actonco2.direct.gov.uk/index.html

Conversion factors These factors are used to determine the carbon dioxide emissions caused by the use of energy. In order to convert energy consumed in kWh to kg of carbon dioxide, the energy use should be multiplied by a conversion factor

Conversion factors are published by the Department for Environment Food and Rural Affairs (**defra**) to supplement the Environmental Reporting Guidelines for Company Reporting on Greenhouse Gas Emissions. They were last published in June 2007, but are due to be updated.

For example;
Conversion factor for natural gas is 0.185kgCO2/kWh
1,000 kWh of gas usage
0.185 x 1000 = **185kg CO2**

Conversion factor for fuel oil is 0.267kgCO2/kWh
1,000 kWh of fuel oil usage
0.267 x 1000 = **267kg CO2**

PART FOUR

4.1 COSTING ASSUMPTIONS

Costs in this guide are for completing the work described as an individual job. They include contractors' overheads, scaffolding, and VAT where applicable. They exclude any temporary works, contingencies and any fees that may be applicable.

The level of costs for the type of work envisaged by this guide is likely to be very sensitive to the context under which the work is procured, the quantity and complexity of the permanent work required and the degree of temporary works needed to achieve it.

The cost of building work is influenced by a wide range of factors, which vary with the individual circumstances of the client, the work, the location and the contractor. No two contractors are likely to charge exactly the same price for an item of work. The information in this guide can therefore only be a reasonable indication of the costs involved in carrying out the work described.

Material and component prices used in this guide are prices for small quantities without trade discounts. Discounts available on manufacturers' list prices will vary from supplier to supplier, and for different purchasers.

The prices contained within this guide are intended to apply to building modifications carried out generally within the United Kingdom (i.e. they are based on a national average level). It will be recognised that price levels vary throughout the United Kingdom. In order to provide some guidance

on regional pricing levels, the regional factors from the BCIS Study of Location Factors are reproduced in Part 4.3. The Study of Location Factors is based on a survey of prices in new building schemes.

The items have been priced individually, that is, as if there was only one item of improvement identified which required action, following a survey.

- The works as a whole will be carried out or managed by a small independent builder or specialist tradesman.

- One item of improvement work will be carried out to a dwelling. Should more than one item of improvement be necessary to a dwelling then there may be cost savings on the rates provided. For example, an elevation may require total window replacement and a wind turbine is to be fitted on that elevation. The scaffolding cost will therefore be reduced, as erecting and dismantling would be included in the guide in both rates.

- The modification work will be procured via some form of competitive process unless it is of a very specialist nature.

- A call out charge has been included in the rates where work is of a minor nature and labour time is less than a full or half day. This rate varies, depending upon the trade, and the appropriate figure is given in the 'Notes' at the bottom of the table in which the call out rate applies.

- The modifications will be carried out in areas of the premises that can be isolated whilst work is carried out, and to which contractors are allowed reasonably clear and unrestricted access.

- The work can be undertaken during normal construction industry working hours.

- Adequate and practical working space will be made available for the execution of the modifications and for the temporary storage of materials and items of equipment.

- Water and domestic power will be provided free of charge.

Although the above criteria set the basis of costs, the prices and estimates in the guide have been compiled to reflect the general nature of modification work, which tends to be small items of work of either a specialist or multi-trade nature, executed at disparate locations within existing premises, generally under less than ideal working conditions.

Savings in on-costs may be achieved where it is possible to arrange for more than one item of repair work to be programmed and undertaken as part of a single repair scheme.

Additional costs may occur in situations where work has to be carried out in areas of the premises that are constantly occupied and cannot be closed off from the occupants, or where operational use has to be preserved. Additional expense cost is also likely where specific constraints are imposed on the contractor, such as restrictions on:

- Access
- Working space
- Storage of materials and equipment
- Removal of debris
- Hours of working
- Noise, dust, vibration
- Method of working, sequencing, phasing etc.

The degree of additional cost will depend on the severity of the constraints imposed and the user of the guide will need to assess their likely effect on both labour productivity and the temporary works needed (see also below) and adjust the estimate they are preparing accordingly.

The quantity and complexity of the modification work to be executed will be significant factors in the cost of the work.

It is likely, with the works envisaged by this guide, that materials and components will often be needed in small quantities. The benefits of economies of scale will therefore be experienced where work can be organised on a scale that allows materials to be purchased in larger volumes.
Where only a very small amount of permanent work is required at one location, its real cost per unit quantity may be significantly higher than it

would be if a larger amount were needed. This is not just because the materials for small volumes of work have to be ordered at 'small quantity' prices but also because the relatively fixed labour costs in travelling to the location, preparation (setting out, positioning materials etc.) and final clearing away are still incurred and can significantly inflate the cost per unit quantity executed. For example, the price for replacing one light switch has included additional charges, as an electrician will be obliged to journey to the location to carry out work that will take a relatively small amount of time. There may be a minimum flat charge of say £50 or £75 for such work (referred to in some contexts as a 'call out charge'). On the other hand, if five or six light switches need to be repositioned then the impact of the 'call out charge' is lessened because it starts to be absorbed by the cost of the greater quantity of work that is required.

The work becomes more complex to carry out if it is in a difficult position (e.g. working at height or on upper floors) with restricted access and lack of working space, or if it is of an exceptionally high standard or quality. The prices and estimates in this guide generally allow for work which could be considered to be of average complexity only, with a range of prices being given in the tables, where relevant, to illustrate normal differences in specified standard or quality.

Where only small quantities of work are required, the fixed cost elements of any temporary works needed (dust screens, protective barriers etc.) can

be a very significant part of the total cost of the work.

The prices and estimates in this guide do not include any allowances for temporary works, other than minor incidental supports and formwork where they are needed in excavation work, forming openings and concrete work. All other temporary work is considered as being part of 'preliminaries'. The exception to this is scaffolding, where costs, when stated, have been included in the tables.

Additions of 20% on labour resource costs and 10% on material and plant resource costs have been made for Establishment Charges (office overheads) and Profit to all prices in this guide. The amounts these percentages generate are thought to be similar to those a prudent contractor would include to cover the costs of running a business and to allow for a reasonable profit.

An allowance of 12% has been made in the prices in this guide for Preliminaries (site overheads). Scaffolding, where required, has been priced additionally.

The extent of preliminaries will depend on the context of the job. They will vary widely according to the specific terms of the contract entered into as well as such criteria as the size, complexity and location of the project; the accessibility of the work; the amount of temporary works required; any restrictions imposed on working hours and practices; the feasibility and degree to which mechanical plant and equipment can be used; safety, health and welfare requirements.

No allowance has been made for Contingencies in the prices or estimates in this guide.

No allowance has been made in the prices and estimates within this guide for any Fees whatsoever.

Generally, the repairs, alterations and adaptations covered by this publication and which are contracted out, are currently subject to VAT. All figures shown in the guide include VAT, at the current standard-rate of 17.5%.

The prices in this guide allow for work to be carried out during normal working hours. Extra cost will be incurred if work needs to be carried out in the evenings or at weekends.

The level of additional costs will vary depending on the working practices of the contractor, but the nationally agreed overtime rates for building workers given in the following table, will give some indication.

Overtime	Basic Rates plus
Weekday or Saturday	
- First four hours	50%
- After first four hours	100%
Sunday	100%
Night Work (Permanent night working)	
Monday – Friday	25%
Weekends	100%

Where the term 'Prime Cost' (or its abbreviation 'PC') is used in this guide in relation to a material or component, the value it refers to represents the list price charged by the supplier excluding VAT, delivery charges and discounts. VAT has been added to the PC in the final rates shown in the tables.

The prices in this guide have been compiled on the basis that normal levels of wastage will be experienced. However, it is possible with the class of work envisaged by this guide that some forms of direct waste would be more difficult to control. Also, a greater than normal amount of indirect waste may occur where only a very small quantity of a material or component is needed, but it can only be supplied in standard can or pack sizes and charged accordingly.

It is probable that debris and waste arising from the type of works envisaged by this guide, will be disposed of by the contractor.

4.2 WHERE TO GET HELP
USEFUL CONTACTS

Professional Bodies

The Royal Institution of Chartered Surveyors, 12 Great George Street, Parliament Square, London SW1P 3AD
Tel: +44 (0)870 333 1600
Fax: +44 (0)207 334 3811
E-mail: contactrics@rics.org
Web site: http://www.rics.org/

RICS Find a Surveyor Service
To find a surveyor in your area:
Tel: +44 (0)870 333 1600
E-mail: contactrics@rics.org
Web site: http://www.ricsfirms.com/

The Royal Institute of British Architects, 66 Portland Place, London W1B 1AD
Tel: +44 (0)906 302 0400
Fax: +44 (0)207 255 1541
Web site: http://www.riba.org/go/RIBA/Home.html

The Institution of Structural Engineers, 11 Upper Belgrave Street, London SW1X 8BH
Tel: +44 (0)207 235 4535
Fax: +44 (0)207 235 4294
Web site: http://www.istructe.org.uk/

The Federation of Master Builders,
Gordon Fisher House, 14-15 Great James Street,
London, WC1N 3DP
Tel: +44 (0)207 242 7583
Fax: +44 (0)207 404 0296
E-mail: central@fmb.org.uk
Web site: http://www.fmb.org.uk/

Energy Conservation Bodies

The Energy Saving Trust
Web site: http://www.energysavingtrust.org.uk/

Department for Business, Enterprise & Regulatory Reform (BERR)
Web site: http://www.lowcarbonbuildings.org.uk/home/

Scottish Community and Householder Renewables Initiative (SCHRI)
Web site: http://www.energysavingtrust.org.uk/schri/

In Northern Ireland grants are available from Reconnect, which is administered by Action Renewables. The Northern Ireland grants were reviewed in March 2008.

Building Research Establishment (BRE)

Bucknalls Lane, Garston, Watford WD25 9XX
Tel: +44 (0)1923 664000
Web site: http://www.bre.co.uk/

Boiler Efficiency and Calculator

SEDBUK – Seasonal Efficiency of Domestic Boilers in the UK
Web site: http://www.sedbuk.com/

Contracts for Building Works

The Joint Contracts Tribunal Limited
Web site: http://www.jctltd.co.uk/
stylesheet.asp?file=492003233614

MW 98: Agreement for Minor Building Work
HG(A) 02: Agreement for Housing Grant Works

Book Shops

RIBA Bookshops
Tel: +44 (0)20 7496 8394
Fax: +44 (0)20 7374 8500
Email: jct@ribabooks.com

RICS Books
Tel: +44 (0)870 333 1600
(press option 2)
Fax: +44 (0)20 7334 3851
Email: licence@rics.org.uk

CIP Limited
Tel: +44 (0)870 078 4400
Fax: +44 (0)870 078 4401
Email: sales@cip-books.com

Builders' Federation

The National Federation of Builders
National Office, 55 Tufton Street, London, SW1P 3QL
Tel: +44 (0)870 8989 091
Fax: +44 (0)870 8989 096
Email: national@builders.org.uk
Web site: http://www.builders.org.uk/nfb/

Trade Federations

Electrical Contractors
The Electrical Contractors' Association (ECA)
ECA Head Office
ESCA House, 34 Palace Court, London, W2 4HY
Tel: +44 (0)20 7313 4800
Fax: +44 (0)20 7221 7344
Web site: http://www.eca.co.uk/

Insulation

National Insulation Association
Tel: +44 (0)1525 383313
Web site: http://www.nationalinsulationassociation.org.uk/

4.3 LOCATION FACTORS

The prices in this guide are average UK prices. The map shows regional pricing factors which indicate the general variability of pricing levels around the country. The factors are taken from the BCIS Study of Location Factors.

Adjusting for Location

The following examples show how to adjust the prices for double glazing a semi detached house, one window.

Install double glazing to casement windows in a semi detached house as Page 81.

£7070

	Factor	£
Scotland	1.04	6010
North West	0.92	5320
North	1.01	5840
Yorkshire & Humberside	0.99	5720
East Midlands	0.94	5430
West Midlands	0.93	5380
Wales	0.96	5550
East Anglia	0.98	5660
South East	1.05	6070
Greater London	1.14	6590
South West	0.98	5660
Northern Ireland	0.67	3870

Scotland
1.04

North
1.01

N.Ireland
0.67

Yorkshire &
Humberside
0.99

North
West
0.92

East Midlands
0.94

West Midlands
0.93

East Anglia
0.98

Wales
0.96

GL
1.14

South West
0.98

South East
1.05

4.4 INFLATION INDICES

The costs in this guide have been priced at 4th quarter 2007.

The table below provides percentage adjustments on the costs of the estimated work from the price level in the guide, to when the work is anticipated to be carried out on site.

Percentages figures all updated from 4Q07

Quarter		Percentage Update
1Q08	(January, February, March)	1.011
2Q08	(April, May, June)	1.022
3Q08	(July, August, September)	1.044
4Q08	(October, November, December)	1.052
1Q09	(January, February, March)	1.059
2Q09	(April, May, June)	1.066
3Q09	(July, August, September)	1.085
4Q09	(October, November, December)	1.089
1Q10	(January, February, March)	1.100
2Q10	(April, May, June)	1.107
3Q10	(July, August, September)	1.125
4Q10	(October, November, December)	1.129

Adjusting for Inflation

The following examples show how to adjust the prices for double glazing a semi detached house, one window.

Install double glazing to casement windows in a semi detached house as Page 81.

£7070

Estimated date construction:	Inflation percentage		Revised project cost
November 2008	(4Q08)	1.052	**£5980**
March 2009	(1Q09)	1.059	**£6020**
September 2010	(3Q10)	1.125	**£6390**

4.5 HOUSE TYPES

The following diagrams have been produced to indicate the types of houses used in the production of various tables in the guide, which give costs for whole house, elevations, floors, rooms etc.

Terraced House

FRONT ELEVATION
GROUND FLOOR AREA 21m²

Semi- Detached House

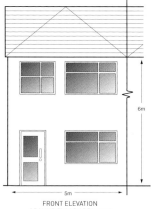

FRONT ELEVATION
GROUND FLOOR AREA 42m²

Detached House

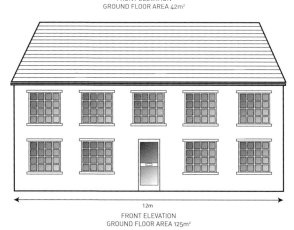

FRONT ELEVATION
GROUND FLOOR AREA 125m²

GLOSSARY

Ancillary works - minor works associated with the installation of the main work item. *For example*, in replacing a boiler some pipework may need to be repositioned to connect to the new boiler and this may also necessitate forming new holes in the wall. Additionally, the old redundant holes for both pipes and boiler fixings will need to be filled in. The repositioning of pipes, forming new holes, and making good to the existing wall, would constitute ancillary works in this example.

Biomass - Fuel produced from organic materials, either from plants or from industrial, commercial, agricultural or domestic products. They do not include fossil fuels, which have taken millions of years to develop.

Cavity Wall – The outside wall of the property, made up of an inner and outer layer or 'skin' with a void (cavity) between, often filled with insulation.

Contingencies or Contingency Sum – A sum of money allowed in your budget, on top of the agreed quote from the contractor, to allow for unforeseen works. An amount, either expressed as a percentage of the work or a lump sum. This will be for work that has not been included in the specification or shown on the drawings, but it may be advisable to allow a figure in case unknown items are encountered.

For example: The works may include replacing some floorboards. However, when the old boards are removed, the joists supporting them may be rotten and require replacing. The contractor will not be aware, until the boards are lifted, that the joists are rotten, and he will therefore not have included a sum in his quote to cover this work.

Distribution Board – A unit containing switches, circuit breakers, fuses etc, which protect the electrical circuits in a property.

Estimate – An approximate price for one part or all of the work. This is sometimes used to mean quotation (see next page).

Fanlight – A window over an internal door to provide natural light into the corridor.

Flush Door – A door that has completely flat faces.

Greywater - Water that is recovered from the property's baths, showers and basins, stored in underground tanks and used for flushing toilets.

Header Tank – A small open cistern (tank) that feeds water to a central heating system.

Insitu – Work that is constructed on site rather than constructed off site and brought into the works.

Ironmongery – Fittings installed to doors and windows to allow them to operate. *For example:* locks, bolts.

Location Factors – Prices for work vary from region to region. The prices in this book are average UK prices and adjustments should be made on estimates for the location of the work.

Making Good – The finishing touches that bring work up to scratch.

PC Sum (Prime Cost Sum) – A sum of money allowed for an item of work or materials supplied by the client. *For example:* installation of a fire alarm system by a specialist already selected by the client, or the cost of a bathroom suite to be purchased by the client.

Photovoltaic Panels - Panels installed on south facing roofs or on the ground, which convert the energy in light to produce electricity.

Photovoltaic Tiles – Tiles which are the same size as traditional roof tiles, installed on south facing roofs to convert the energy in light to produce electricity.

Plasterboard – Prefabricated sheets of plaster, which are used for walls and ceilings.

Prefabricated – An item of the works made off site and brought onto the site. *For example:* roof truss.

Preliminaries – These are costs for items that are required to carry out the contract other than the actual construction costs. *For example:* travelling costs, the hire of scaffolding or other items of plant (e.g. cement mixers), office and other administrative charges.

Provisional Sum – An amount included in the contract sum/agreed quote for additional works that are not fully specified. *For example:* fitted units to a bedroom are required but the design/materials are not finalised at the time the contract is agreed. By inserting a reasonable sum, the contractor can allow for his overheads and include these works into his programme.

Quote/Quotation – The price offered by the contractor to do the work.

Render – A coating of cement and sand applied to the face of an external wall.

Retention – A sum of money set aside by the client (you) from the contract sum until the works are completed to your satisfaction.

Ring Main – The power circuit for electrical sockets in the property.

Screed – A layer of fine concrete, which is used to provide a smooth surface prior to laying a floor finish.

Sill – The bottom horizontal member of a door or window frame.

Skim – The thin finishing coat of plaster that provides a smooth finish for decoration etc.

Solar Panels – Panels installed on south facing roofs or on the ground, which collect the sun's energy and convert it to heat water.

Solar Tiles – Tiles which are the same size as traditional roof tiles, installed on south facing roofs to collect the sun's energy and convert it to heat water.

Stack – The vertical pipe that carries waste water from toilets, baths, sinks etc to the drainage system.

Trap – A curved section of drain that holds water and provides a seal that prevents any odours returning into the room.

TRV – Thermostatic radiator valve. This valve regulates the temperature of the radiator.

Valuations - These are assessments of work completed by certain agreed dates during construction of larger projects. The assessment of work shall be calculated from the sums included in the contract and the agreed dates shall be laid out in the Contract. *For example:* fortnightly payments - valuations shall be undertaken every two weeks. Variations, where occurring, will also be included in these Valuations. Payments shall be made to the contractor based on those valuations.

Variations – These are work items that arise during the construction that were not allowed for in the quote. *For example:* during replacement of some floor boards, the joists below are found to be rotten. The quote only allowed for replacing the boards, the replacement of the joists is therefore a variation.

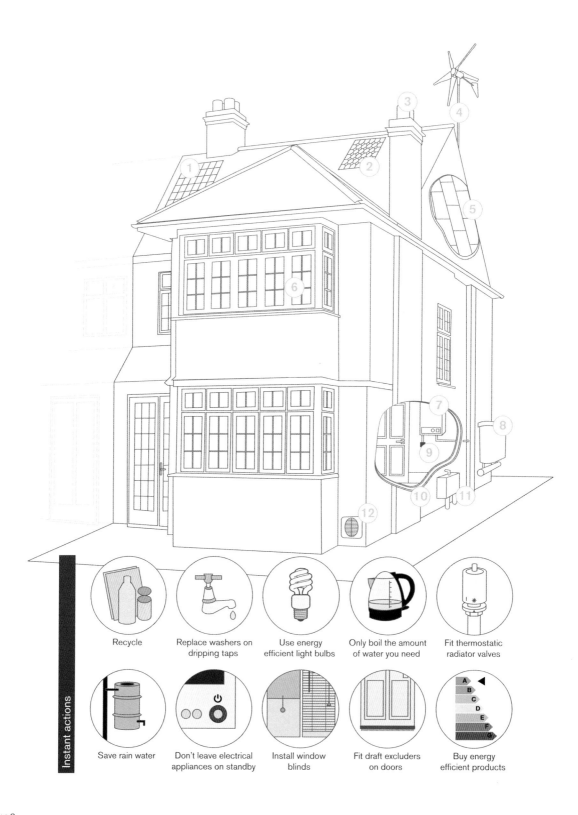

Instant actions

Recycle

Replace washers on dripping taps

Use energy efficient light bulbs

Only boil the amount of water you need

Fit thermostatic radiator valves

Save rain water

Don't leave electrical appliances on standby

Install window blinds

Fit draft excluders on doors

Buy energy efficient products

Big actions

1 Solar hot water
Solar energy can be used to heat water without harmful greenhouse gas emissions

2 Photovoltaics
A photovoltaic cell converts light energy into electrical energy that can power domestic appliances

3 Bio-mass Energy
Biomass energy comes from burning biological material which has been converted into a form suitable for domestic incineration

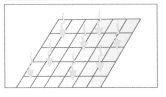
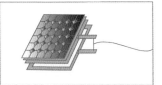

4 Wind turbine
Wind turbines are designed to generate electricity from wind power

5 Re-roof and insulation / loft insulation
Loft insulation acts as a blanket, trapping heat rising from the house below

6 Double & Triple glazing
The air space between the two layers of glass both insulates the room and reduces heat loss through a window

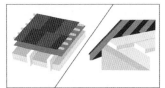
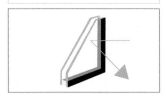

7 Condensing Boiler
This type of boiler recovers waste heat that conventional boilers vent into the atmosphere

8 Grey water
Collecting, treating and recycling grey water from household use, such as domestic appliances, baths and showers

9 Micro CHP (Combined heat and power)
Cogeneration of heat and power in a single domestic system

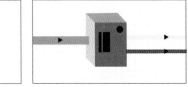

10 Wall & cavity Insulation
Provides insulation and reduces heat loss through outside walls

11 Ground Source Heat Pump
This uses the ground as either a heat source, when operating in heating mode, or a heat sink, when operating in cooling mode

12 Heat recovery ventilation
Heat generated in one part of the house is used to warm fresh air being delivered to another

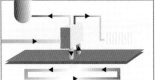

INDEX